What Do You Know About Ritual?

What Do You Know About Ritual?

The Complete Mason's Commentary

Revd. Neville Barker Cryer

Lewis  Masonic

First published 2008
Reprinted 2010, 2017
This impression 2020

ISBN 978 085318 271 9

Published by Lewis Masonic
an imprint of Ian Allan Publishing Ltd, Shepperton, Middx Tw17 8AS.

Printed in England.

Visit the Lewis Masonic website at:
www.lewismasonic.com

CONTENTS

1
Introduction

It must be 55 years ago that the idea for this kind of book first came into my mind. I had moved once more with my professional occupation to my home city of Manchester and had been introduced to a new lodge there by one of my churchwardens, the local doctor. In Wolseley Lodge No. 1993 I soon discovered that having to wait to get on the ladder of promotion provided no sinecure. Master Masons without a job in office were given the task of learning the Emulation catechetical lectures and then reciting the answers in open lodge with another non-officer Past Master in the Chair asking the questions. One was by no means left hanging around wondering what to do and what Freemasonry was all about.

I began to see the point of so much that I heard in the degree ceremonies. What I also realised, however, was that there were more things in the ceremonies that the lectures did not explain. Surely, I thought, there is a need for that too to be done. Of course, I was far too junior to attempt such a thing and in those days there was still a great deal of resistance to the notion of producing information about the Craft that was not included in the approved rituals, including the explanatory lectures. A commitment to progressing through many degrees, and then serving as a Grand Officer and ruler, meant that these early ideas had to be put on hold.

Happily those days of undue 'secrecy' and lack of real instruction are now over. Journeying throughout our land and speaking to countless groups of modern Masons has convinced me that there is in many quarters a real thirst for Masonic knowledge that is not being, or even able to be, met. Questions following talks, letters through my door and even requests on the phone all convince me that there is a market for commentary on the regular ceremonies that a Mason will go through or watch continually.

In my lifetime that commentary could have been supplied by countless Preceptors, and has by some, but the emphasis has tended to be on correct performance of the ritual rather than on its equally important significance. Too many brethren know the words but are either ignorant of, or perplexed by, what they are in fact saying. That is not only the case in Freemasonry. It is the reason why there are usually sermons in a church service. The faithful need help in understanding what they read or say.

In Freemasonry we now have other circumstances that seem to suggest why commentaries such as these may be of some advantage. The reduction in the number of candidates can mean that there are occasions for meeting when the usual progressive ceremonies are not available. That is an excellent opportunity for either a lecture or the rehearsal of a degree. Yet the mere repetition of those well-known words does not in itself increase our knowledge about them. It is in order to have such occasions 'with a difference' that the papers in this book are here offered. They have been tried in several places and found to be helpful. We still recall the ceremony but now we begin to appreciate what it is teaching and the tradition that it seeks to preserve. It is something to which visitors can be invited and which they too could be encouraged to try. If the lodge has plenty of candidates then this is a method for instructing them in further points when they come for rehearsal. It is above all the means of enabling Freemasons to make a daily advancement in Masonic knowledge. That has been my intention throughout.

A word must certainly be said about the title of this book. After nearly 60 years in the practice of the Craft I have not the slightest hesitation in asserting that if time, opportunity and means are available one ought to have enjoyed the ceremonies commented on here to be what one might call a complete English Freemason. As one who is in many other Orders this is not in any way to suggest that other parts of Masonry are unnecessary or of less value. What I am being told constantly is that Freemasons today have more limited time and resources at their disposal. If that is true then what I am proposing here is that if a brother wants to get to the heart of Masonry and can only do so much, then these ceremonies are the ones to which he needs to belong. Traditionally these are the oldest, the most cohesive and most certain to provide a 21st century Mason with all that he really ought to know. It is no less a fact that if you are not a member of these degrees or orders then you are not able to apply for the rest.

I therefore commend these pages to my English brethren. Some of what I have written elsewhere forms part of these in context and is offered to a wider audience. It is the hope of the author that it may enable some to enjoy their Masonry more and for others to taste some pleasures that they may just not have known were there.

2

Commentary on the First Degree Ceremony

This form of presentation of the ceremony starts with the knocks on the door by the Tyler and the Inner Guard's report to the Master. On this occasion the obligation can be taken as read and in the questioning at the Wardens' places afterwards only the S. W's queries need be used. This form of the ceremony ends before the Charge to the Initiate. No one present takes any part in the ceremony except the designated officers. Everyone else remains seated throughout. What follows below are the points at which an appointed Commentator calls for a 'Pause' whilst an explanation is given of what has just taken place. Between each pause, of course, work resumes.

1st Pause: After having had the candidate vouched for by the Tyler and when the Inner Guard has reported to the Worshipful Master.

Commentary: It may surprise many English Masons to realise that the words, 'by the help of God, being free and of good report', twice repeated already, are the password leading to the First Degree. Indeed, if you want to enter any Lodge in Bristol today these are the words that you have to speak to the Deacon standing just inside the lodge door. In an Irish lodge you will be asked for them during the Opening. They also remind us that it was once the case that an unprompted profession of belief in a Deity, one's status locally as a Freeman, and two written testimonies as to good character were needed before Initiation could be allowed.

2nd Pause: After the Worshipful Master has spoken to the candidate regarding his free status and age and the candidate has replied.

Commentary: The presentation of a sharp instrument to the breast of the candidate is part of the ancient practice of testing a candidate's five senses. We know he can hear what is said to him because he replies; we know he could see if not hood-winked; we know he can use his limbs to move about, and now we know he can feel. The instrument originally used to prick his breast was a trowel but this was later changed to a dagger or poignard. Further, the candidate had once to have been an apprentice for 7 years from the age of 14 and so was now of the full age of 21 years. He had also to have served his articles so as to be able to be a Freeman of the Borough in some trade so that he could join the Masons' Lodge that was attached to their Guild. Even when such requirements were no longer needed the candidate had still to be a free man and so able to take and fulfil an obligation.

3rd Pause: When the candidate has got to his feet after hearing the Worshipful Master say, '...we trust no danger can ensue.'

Commentary: Every candidate is expected to have his own religious beliefs so that Freemasonry cannot be an alternative and conflicting religion. As every Freemason professes a belief in a Supreme Being it is right that there should be prayer to the Deity, but in such prayer each Mason addresses the Deity of his choice. We need also to be reminded that from medieval times the motto on the banner of the Masons' Guild was 'In God is all our trust'. Now you can see why the question put just now to the candidate was phrased as it was.

4th Pause: At the point where, on the first perambulation, the candidate has struck the Junior Warden on the right shoulder, but before the Junior Warden speaks.

Commentary: Originally the candidate was led round a centre table where the brethren sat so that they could see him even though he could not see them. As he passed round they would check that he was a 'fit and proper person' to be received, i.e. that he was male because his breast was exposed; that, as in a modern airport check, he had no metal items on him for use as a weapon; and was so penniless that he needed an old slipper lent by this, his mother lodge, to wear. As he came round the back of the seated brethren it was logical that as he needed to attract the attention of the Junior Warden he should strike him on his right, or nearest, shoulder. '

5th Pause: At the point where the Senior Warden has presented the candidate as being 'properly prepared to be made a Mason' but before the Worshipful Master responds.

Commentary: The preparation required of an English Mason today is fairly mild as compared with what was required formerly, or as is still the case in some continental Grand Lodges. I have already mentioned written reports about his previous conduct (as still required in Scandinavia), and other previous requirements have included a doctor testing him for fitness; the candidate sitting down for an hour alone in a candle-lit room and writing down why he wished to become a Mason (as still happens in Scandinavia and parts of Germany); and the candidate stripping completely to put on special clothing (as still happens in some of our own older English lodges). You can see why we still use the term in our ritual 'properly prepared', as we do. Do most of us today get off too lightly?

6th Pause: At the end of the three questions put to the candidate by the Worshipful Master and when the candidate has thrice said, 'I do'.

Commentary: Once again an enquiry is made of the candidate regarding his desire to receive 'the mysteries and privileges of Freemasonry'. In operative times these were, of course, very real and very important. The 'mysteries' were trade secrets and practices that only those who were bona fide apprentices were allowed to learn and then apply in the stonemason's art. The 'privileges' were those of being recognised as legitimate tradesmen who could earn wages by offering a special skill and also become a member of the Masons' Guild. This then meant that you were able to be part of a city or town government, which was a profitable privilege indeed. What 'mysteries and privileges' are for Accepted Masons we shall learn shortly.

7th Pause: At the point where the candidate has taken the steps leading him to the pedestal for obligation, and before the Worshipful Master speaks to him.

Commentary: There is a real possibility that we can misunderstand what a candidate is doing here. It may be thought that what makes his steps irregular is taking ones which are of different lengths or taken in a peculiar manner. But that is not the case. All a man's steps of any kind are irregular until he has taken an obligation to keep the rules (regulae) of our Institution. Before he does this there is no proper way for any candidate to approach the East. Any steps the Lodge requires are irregular at this point. Only after he has taken his obligation will the candidate take a first regular step. We should therefore never query what other lodges require when telling candidates to move East at this stage. Whatever they lay down doesn't prevent his steps from being irregular.

8th Pause: When the candidate is kneeling at the pedestal ready to take his obligation but before the Worshipful Master knocks.

Commentary: Freemasons here prepare to follow an ancient tradition. Evidence from at least 1390 shows that guild masons knelt and laid a hand on a book before taking an obligation to be true and faithful. Many still give such an undertaking as those in court, holding a book, and those in posts of special government trust have to give their sincere assent to keep official secrets to themselves. This is all that the candidate is preparing to do here, only in this case he also holds one of the implements of the old trade.

Remember: the first and last sentences only of the obligation need be used.

9th Pause: After the Worshipful Master has said to the candidate, 'You will seal it with your lips on the V. S. L.'

Commentary: The requirement in the obligation not to write or print may surprise today's candidates because they will soon find themselves presented with a ritual book from which they will have to learn, and are also encouraged to be open with non-Masons about what they practise here.

However, the reciting of such an undertaking is one of the oldest points of Masonic ritual and reflects a time when any speaking or writing of ritual was utterly forbidden. It may not be known that the first official ritual book printed in England only came out in the mid-19th century and the Grand Lodge of Pennsylvania still does not allow any printed ceremonial texts to be used. There the brethren who are to assume office have to learn the ritual face-to-face with each other in a closed room.

10th Pause: At the point where the Worshipful Master has brought the candidate to his feet after the words, 'Rise, newly obligated Brother among Masons.'

Commentary: It is very fitting that as the blindfold is removed the candidate's attention should be directed to the Volume of the Sacred Law on which he has just taken his obligation. This is true whether it be the Holy Bible or some other sacred text that may have been laid upon it. It is in the Bible that we read how at the creation of the world God said, 'Let there be light and there was light'. This phrase is now given a special place in a later stage of our Masonic progress but it is also fitting for this moment. This is also the point where Masons can be reminded of a useful tip: whenever a candidate kneels everyone else stands, and when the candidate rises all save the necessary officers sit. That applies to any degree.

11th Pause: At the point in the entrusting where the Worshipful Master says, '...what that word is: it is B . . z' and he, the Junior Deacon and the candidate spell it.

Commentary: We have now reached what can be regarded as the heart of the Initiation. Based on the assurances given in the obligation the Worshipful Master proceeds to entrust the candidate with the secrets of the degree. It is here that we see the greatest difference between the old working practices of the actual stonemasons and the new customs of the Free & Accepted Masons. The old 'secrets' were the methods of carrying out the work of erection that only trained and qualified Apprentices could learn. Since such 'real work' is no longer involved, the secrets here refer to the means by which those who once came seeking work on a building site were tested and approved. We should also note that all the footsteps now taken by the new Freemason are at last 'regular' because of his new status. The proper form of such steps is in the shape of a Tau Cross, that can only be explained fully later in his Masonic progress.

12th Pause: At the point after his interrogation when the Senior Warden says, 'Pass, B . . z'.

Commentary: The enquiry through which the candidate has just passed is all that remains of a much longer 18th Century procedure. It was then the custom for the candidate to be sat at the table after his obligation and there he listened to an exchange of questions and answers, not only between the Worshipful Master and his Wardens but sometimes with all the members of the Lodge in turn. In America to this day something of the same happens as the Right Worshipful Master puts questions to one or more of the officers about all that has taken place so far, e. g. why the candidate was blindfolded; why slipshod; why paraded round the room and so on. All that was dropped following the Union of English Grand Lodges in 1813 because it was thought that it would unduly prolong the ceremony. It was more instructive, however, than merely testing a step, a grip and a password. We are now less well-informed.

13th Pause: At the point where the Senior Warden has invested the candidate with his first apron and handed him back to the Junior Deacon to face the Worshipful Master.

Commentary: The candidate has now received an apron and can feel at last that he is really one of the Brethren. In England today we think of this plain white apron as belonging only to an Apprentice but for most brethren in the 18th Century this was the normal apron which all Masons wore. In America you will still find a pile of plain white aprons in the anteroom for use by members or guests though not lodge officers. The plain white apron reminds us that we are all equal, for it was from this item that all our clothing took its rise. The white apron is still there below all the other decoration that has been added.

14th Pause: The candidate having been placed in the north-east corner and when the Junior Deacon has said, 'Pay attention to the Worshipful Master'.

Commentary: One of the reasons why Freemasonry became so popular in the 17th Century for men who were not stonemasons was because it was a society where men of different religious or political opinions could meet as equals and brothers. That is why the Worshipful Master has just emphasised the need for us to remember what we are doing when we put on our aprons for a lodge meeting. If we cannot meet as amicable brethren then we are not to put on an apron.

The new Mason may next wonder why he has to stand with his feet at a right angle facing the centre when his attention is drawn to the Master in the East. It is because his feet should be round a rough stone placed at this corner, as is still the custom in some old English lodges. Moreover, the Worshipful Master would originally have been in front of him at a table in the centre and not away in the East.

15th Pause: When the Worshipful Master has finished his address to the candidate with the words, '...practising that virtue you have professed to admire.'

Commentary: The new Mason can now understand why he was placed in this part of the lodge room. It was originally the north-east part of a sacred building. But why, we may ask, was the north-east corner chosen as the place for the first or foundation stone? The answer is that in all medieval churches this was where the Easter sepulchre, a symbolic tomb of Christ was set and from here the first light of Easter came. Easter proclaimed the great promise of God's love and care for his people and that fits well with the stress on charity and brotherly love of which the Worshipful Master speaks.

When the new Mason is then asked for alms he would once have been presented with a trowel, flat side upwards, because that was the symbol of brotherly love and care. That, you now see, is why, when the Grand Lodge created the office of Charity Steward, the trowel was re-introduced as his jewel. The new Mason would also have been unprompted as to what to say to a request for alms so that, having to reply without help, this moment would forever be imprinted on his memory.

16th Pause: When the tools have been presented and the words, '...members of regularly organised society' have been spoken.

Commentary: Another of the most obvious differences between Operative and Accepted Freemasonry is this explanation of the symbolic meaning of the working tools. As a great Secretary of Quatuor Coronati Lodge, Brother Harry Carr, once remarked, 'You won't find this ritual in medieval masonry.' He did not mean that allegory and symbolism did not then exist but that the mason's tools were so essential for day-to-day labour, as our explanation indeed says, that they would not be thought of in any other way. For us it is different.

Notice, by the way, that whilst the tools should speak to us of service to others and the value of education, they no less stress prayer to Almighty God and the need of a clear conscience so that God may accept our thoughts and deeds. Anyone who claims that a clear awareness of God is missing from the Craft degrees has perhaps not appreciated what we say in the ritual.

17th Pause: After the Worshipful Master has given the candidate his various booklets and told him that a Charge will follow when he returns, finishing with the words, '...the excellencies of the Institution and the qualifications of its members'.

Commentary: As we come to the close of this presentation we need, like the Apprentice, to be reminded of three important matters. The first is to appreciate the background and history of the lodge to which we belong. The Warrant not only authorises the holding of our meetings but tells us when and how we began such meetings and to whom we are indebted for our Lodge existence. Do read it if you haven't.

Our Grand Lodge Constitutions give us all the information we need to explain what Freemasonry is and how it functions. Why not dip into it regularly? Our bye-laws tell us how to be good members of our own lodge. For a long time in England the bye-laws had to be read out regularly in open Lodge and at least once a year. That is no longer required because we are supposed to be able to read them for ourselves, so let us do that for each other's sake.

If we were to make full use of all these items that are now made available to us what useful and informed brethren we would be. We would even be more ready than some are for the Second Degree. Indeed, in some lodges, the questions to be answered before that degree can be conferred are rehearsed, by the Worshipful Master and one of his officers, at a point before the First Degree is closed. In this way the candidate can both hear and become accustomed to what he has to learn. Real tradition, you know, when understood, can be a great thing.

3

Commentary on the Charge After Initiation

All of us soon become familiar with the words which we will hear delivered at the end of an Initiation ceremony. In due course one of us will, or will already have had to, learn those words as an officer of a lodge and when that happens we might begin to wonder afresh what exactly it is that we have been required to say to a new member of the Craft. What I want to do for a few moments is to reflect on those words, not, of course, with any idea of increasing the number of words we already use but thinking a little more deeply about what we could learn from this Charge if we were in a real lodge of Instruction that taught us the meaning of ritual and not just its rehearsal. What is now shared with you is something of what we ought to have in mind whenever we, or another, delivers it.

What is clear from the start of the charge is that we have not now joined a group of working masons. The very words 'ceremony', 'admitted a member', and 'honourable Society' all point out the difference between those working on a building site and others who are now formally accepted into a special social group that has little or nothing to do with practical building work. When, therefore, we are told that our Society is ancient, as 'having subsisted from time immemorial' we are not to think of Egyptian, Greek or Roman stonemasons, nor even of medieval or Knight Templar craftsmen, for they were of a different type to ourselves.

When we speak of Time Immemorial we go back to the reign of Elizabeth I when the better-off freemasons had what we call a 'guild', and were now admitting to that guild those from other trades who were Freemen of the local city or borough like themselves. Being masons the guild had a lodge and as these other tradesmen joined that lodge they were described as being 'accepted'. It is from that development that we get the title 'Free and Accepted' which is how we are known to this day. When you hear the word 'ancient' it is to those days in the 16th and 17th Centuries that we refer. Members of the four lodges in 1717 would have known this very well. It is why they so much wanted to preserve their ancient Society.

We are next told that this is an honourable Society. Let me point out at once that what makes it honourable is not any special status or privilege but the fact that its members put into practice the good intentions that are drawn to their attention in it. This is a fundamental point about Freemasonry. Just as it is one thing to be aware of what a hammer and chisel are for, but quite another to be able to use them to carve a stone in a building, so there is also a real difference between saying what is good and right and putting it into practice. Our honourable society depends on each of us being ready and willing to carry out its precepts. Here we can learn from what we are to do in lodge. If we do not try to carry out what the lodge preceptor asks us to do for our ceremonies then it is all a waste of time. Outside in ordinary life, as well as in the lodge, we shall be honourable as we carry out what our Masonic precepts seek to teach us. We shall not become honourable just because we are members. That is why we are told that the 'foundation' of our Craft is solid when there is seen to be the 'practice of every moral and social virtue'. Words have to become deeds.

On the basis of what Freemasonry displays we are next told that even kings have not been unwilling to enter this Society and take the humblest position. This is what is meant by the words, 'exchange the sceptre for the trowel'. The trowel today is seen as the jewel attached to the collar of the Charity Steward who is the person who is meant to care for the members. The trowel was appointed to be worn there, not too long ago, because it had in earlier times been the symbol of care for the brotherhood and that which secured the well-being of the brethren. This was seen in the 18th Century when there was no office of Inner Guard and the latest initiate to the lodge was the one who was on the inside of the door when the next candidate was to be admitted. Since each initiate was given a trowel as well as an apron it was with a trowel that the guardian of the door answered the knocks there and also pricked the flesh of the next candidate. It was thus that the trowel came to acquire the quality of making sure that only fit men were admitted and the security of the lodge was maintained. Here the mention of a trowel means that whilst the ruler of a kingdom was entitled to wield a sceptre as the top person in the land, when he entered Freemasonry he had to be ready to become the lowliest member for a time. It is a lesson that all Freemasons must learn. Every time you join another branch of Masonry you have to start at the bottom of a ladder again.

Our attention is now turned to the Volume of the Sacred Law. Here we are to remember that in English Freemasonry such a volume has to be present before we begin, and remain open whilst the lodge work is done. In fact the version of the Volume of the Sacred Law that is needed at all times with us is the whole English Bible. If any candidate wishes to take his obligations on another sacred book he may, of course, do so but that other version must be on, or beside, the Bible. It is the constant presence of the Volume of the Sacred Law that principally dictates whether a lodge you may be visiting is regular and therefore one which you and I can attend, in our own country or elsewhere. If there is no open sacred book on the pedestal of a lodge you attend then you should not be there.

Whilst we are taught that the Volume of the Sacred Law contains teaching that is to be our 'unerring' guide I want you to notice that what I said earlier is still the rule. The Bible is not there to be just a token but is 'to regulate your actions'. Having the Volume of the Sacred Law present is not for appearance's sake. It is meant to be the assurance that those who gather round it are those who live by its guidance. That is why the object of all our Freemasonry is summed up by the Hebrew words 'Holiness to the Lord', written below the representation of the Ark of the Covenant on a Master Mason's certificate which we are all meant to receive eventually. Our whole life is to show where we take our stand and this Charge now spells that out.

We start, where I have just said that we finish, with the Lord God at the centre of our life. This is to remind you at the end of the Initiation ceremony of where we began. We are all asked, 'In all cases of difficulty and danger in whom do you put your trust?' The answer you should have given freely is 'In God'. It may interest you to know that that affirmation too is ancient because when the stonemasons had a Guild it would have had its own banner and on that were inscribed the words, 'In Domino spero', that means 'In the Lord is my trust'. So here we are again being called upon to respect the very name of God by the way we speak of him, whether frustrated or not, by remembering that here is the source of our very existence; by asking for his help in all legitimate business and turning to him in moments of distress. May I suggest that if we Masons really put these words into practice, in a world in which a university professor has just produced a book called The God Delusion, then we will indeed continue to be a very distinctive group in society.

The call to serve our neighbour could be equally distinctive at a time when self-interest seems to be very much the common motivation for people's behaviour. Charity in its fullest sense has always been an especial mark of Masons and it is only right that through the office of the Charity Steward we have someone who can help us 'relieve the necessities of others' and 'soothe others' afflictions'. This does not mean that we do not have to put ourselves out in our private lives to serve in these ways but at least the regular report by our lodge representatives can keep this aspect of our Masonic commitment freshly before us. The similarity of the last sentence at this point to the second of the great Bible commandments in the Book of Deuteronomy, to love our neighbour as we love ourselves, cannot escape our notice.

The third pointer here, which has to do with our own wellbeing, echoes the requirements of the original mason-workman who had to take care of himself physically and mentally. He had to do this so that he could discharge the work that he was engaged to do. Notice that in addition to being fit, which for us has something to do with food, drink and exercise, we are also to keep our minds active so that we can share with our brethren and our local community the talents that we are born with but which need developing. May I remind you that we are one of the few Institutions in this country that encourages its members to use their memory for the retention and expression of knowledge. The learning of ritual is an offshoot of the days when the Mystery Plays were produced, by the masons amongst other trades, and it was thought that what was said in those plays, that were based on the Bible, was so sacred and important that it had to be correctly spoken. The players who forgot their lines or got them wrong were fined. Let us be grateful that that imposition no longer applies amongst us but let us no less realise that our lines still deserve to be well memorised.

As this Charge turns to our duties as citizens we should remember our origins in the Freemen's guilds of each city or town. The guild owed its authority to a charter from the King and it is thus only right that we, their descendants, should reaffirm our allegiance to the monarch of the land where we live. Our Freemasonry had early to suffer the divisions caused by the 17th century Civil War when allegiance to a rightful monarch was a matter of life and death. In an age which is all too aware of plots and disturbances of the peace it is only right that we should be known to be those who are peaceable and law-abiding. I have never forgotten the words of a London policeman: 'I come to lodge with relief knowing that for once I am not going to be in the company of rogues and robbers.' That is a standard which we ought strenuously to preserve.

So we turn again, as we did earlier, to the matter of our private behaviour. It is here that we come to what some Masons may consider an intrusion too far in what could otherwise be thought of as an ordinary club activity. Can you imagine a Rotary, Lions, or golf club 'recommending the practice of every domestic as well as public virtue'. Yet the old tradition from which we stem involved its members in both these spheres. A Master was responsible for the whole conduct of his apprentices, that they would not gamble nor get drunk, but also that they would not behave improperly with his wife, daughter, sister or even housemaid. An apprentice was to be on time at meals, decent in dress, polite to customers and respectful to his superiors. There is even an echo of this side of a young mason's behaviour in a later obligation when we promise to 'strictly respect the chastity of… his wife, his sister and his child'. In our modern situation we are being reminded that what we do in our private lives can have an effect on everyone else in our organisation. Now you can perhaps see why some brethren have to be tried and excluded when their public or private behaviour brings us all into disrepute.

If you are restrained in your desires by Prudence; curbed in your appetites by Temperance; strengthened to sustain injustice or disappointment by Fortitude, and enabled to deal fairly with others by a sense of Justice, you will be both a credit to yourself and a benefit to the brotherhood. In the light of what was said above about serving our neighbours it is surely not necessary to say more about charity and caring.

Thus we turn to the great matters of confidentiality, trustworthiness and cooperation. Our great movement began with men whose keeping of special trade secrets was the guarantee of their livelihood. That idea spread in the guild to a whole new range of matters: how wages were set; how a guild or lodge ruler was to be selected; who received charity and why; what was to be in their Charges; and so much more. When some of us joined Masonry secrecy was very extensive but nowadays we are told that only the modes of recognition, passwords and signs merit careful control though there are also matters discussed in each lodge which are relevant to those members only and are not for general information.

What is important still and is now brought to our attention is that if we want to enjoy our Masonry to the full then we will appreciate each new degree or Order if we wait to be initiated into it and don't try to find out about its ceremonies before then. You can be well assured that being patient until your blindfold is removed or a story unfolds is far and away the best way to proceed when you join any other degrees. That not only proves your trustworthiness but allows you time to set each part in its true place in Freemasonry as a whole.

The other proof of your trustworthiness is certainly in the matter of recommending candidates. Of course we need candidates in order to survive but we do not need them at any price. When you or I are approached and asked by someone, or even feel impelled to suggest the Craft to another, let us at least first have imagined that person standing where the recipient of this Charge would stand and ask the question, is he someone who will happily respond to this list of requirements or do they just not fit his character? That is the least you owe him in giving him your vote of confidence. What is most important is that you do really know him. I can recall very early on in my time as a Mason being an onlooker over a cup of tea when a member of the lodge I was attending asked their Grand Officer if he would second a candidate. 'You will have seen him at two Ladies' evenings', he said, 'and I have known him three years.'

'Really', said the Grand Officer, 'and is he married?'

'Yes', said the expectant proposer. 'Have they any children?'

'I think so.'

'What is his job?'

'I have never asked him.'

'Would his wife be happy if he joined?'

'I don't know.'

'Well', said the Grand Officer, 'until you know him and his family a lot better don't propose him or I will have to black ball him.'

A lodge has to be able to trust its members if we are to have the right candidates. If you propose anyone let it always be a happy experience. If you ever have a disappointing candidate it will teach you how right this charge can be.

No lodge can operate unless its members cooperate in what it is decided to do. Get into the habit from the start of putting down all your lodge's dates in your diary for the next year. When the summons comes answer it as soon as you can and if you are an officer and will not be able to get there make that clear at once. That is what is meant by a 'prompt attention to all signs and summonses'. You are here pledging yourself to obey and the easiest way is to do it at once. For just consider how upset you would be if the Secretary didn't bother to prepare and send out the summons, book the hall or order dinner. If he does his bigger task then who are you and I to forget to make one reply? This charge is not about words. It is about deeds as has been constantly repeated throughout this commentary.

I will not expand, though I am tempted, on the matter of behaviour in the lodge and attention to what the Master and Wardens are trying to do. One day we may all be in that position and we will want all the attention that others can give us. What is most important is to realise that as we gather in lodge we are in one of the few places in this country where people of different political and religious views can meet without being embarrassed or angry. We need to keep it that way.

This Charge closes with yet another intrusion into our private life by encouraging us to have such hobbies and interests as will ensure that we are decent folk to know, able to be of use locally or nationally, and men who add to the lustre and reputation of Freemasonry. In this connection it is the seven Liberal Arts and Sciences that we are specially to start, or to continue, studying. If you don't know what that covers then either just wait for the second degree tracing board explanation or ask an experienced brother in the lodge. If you want to know how important those Arts and Sciences have been in ancient Masonry then read another book of mine that is called 'York Mysteries Revealed'.

I now hope that as a result of what I have shared with you, you have already seen how valuable it is to make a daily advancement in Masonic knowledge which entails more than just learning the ritual. May you have realised, above all else, that this Charge needs not only to be imprinted on your heart but made to come alive in your daily lives so that when folk know you to be a Mason they will recognise the qualities that have here been outlined. I also hope that one day you will in turn pass on your ideas and thoughts on the First Degree charge to the next generation.

4

Commentary on the Second Degree Ceremony

This presentation of the ceremony begins with the Tyler's knock on the door and the Inner Guard's report to the Worshipful Master. Only the first and last sentences of the obligation are used but we have the affirmation and sealing with the lips on the Volume of the Sacred Law. There need only be one interrogation, that by the Senior Warden, after the sign, token and grip have been given. This form of ceremony ends before an explanation of the Tracing Board. No one present takes any part in the ceremony except the designated officers and so all but they remain seated throughout. What follows are the points when there is a 'Pause' whilst an explanation is given of what has just taken place.

1st Pause: After the Tyler's words to the Inner Guard ending with 'for which ceremony he is properly prepared'.

Commentary: Before an Apprentice could become a Fellow or Master of the Craft in operative times his progress was marked by his seven years of indentured service. He had several special tasks to complete and a standard he had to reach. Today we might well wonder what progress had indeed been made since this Apprentice was initiated. What has he learnt of the Craft and begun to do other than memorise some answers to a few questions? Does he even understand these? Have we become too accustomed to automatic advancement? In many European lodges a candidate for this degree has to sit down and write out something of what he has learnt thus far in Freemasonry.

2nd Pause: Where the Inner Guard has reported to the Worshipful Master and after the Worshipful Master has asked, 'Do you, Brother Inner Guard, vouch that he is in possession of the password?'

Commentary: Notice that to attain the privileges of the second degree we need God's help since by our own unaided effort we will fail. This is a spiritual lesson that is easily overlooked but which pervades all English Masonry. Whilst the one implement presented to the candidate's breast was meant to touch the conscience, here the Square reminds us of the need for the skill, both manual and mental, which a fully trained apprentice would be expected to be able to use. For us it will speak of the need to act 'on the square' with all mankind. About the Password more will be said shortly.

3rd Pause: When the candidate has risen after Prayer.

Commentary: Once the candidate has given the necessary proof of being a Mason the first activity in which he shares is prayer. Note that the emphasis is on the dependence, not only of the candidate but of all the brethren, upon God's aid in our work. That, after all, was what was said was true when we first came into a lodge. Moreover, we are here reminded that the precepts we are to follow are not those of men but God's. The emphasis on divine power and purposes in all our labours reflects the old Guild Masons' banner that bore the words, 'In God is all our trust'.

4th Pause: After the dialogue with the Junior Warden when the latter says, 'Pass, B . . z'.

Commentary: In the Guild Masonry of the 17th Century, as still in Irish working today, every individual Mason had to be questioned for passwords before a lodge could be opened in a new degree. This is reflected in what we have just seen take place. But there is more.

Originally, in Moderns lodges, each of the Wardens sat in the West beside a pillar near the lodge entrance, guarding the 'gate' of the lodge. When the first and second degree ceremonies were created out of the old

Fellows degree one pillar was attached to each ceremony. When the Junior Warden says, 'Pass B . . z' he is really saying, 'You are permitted to pass my part of the lodge gate'. Shortly the candidate will 'Pass J . . . n' and thus gain full access to a Lodge of Fellows, in operative times the only kind of lodge there was.

5th Pause: After the dialogue with the Senior Warden when the latter has said, 'Pass Sh . . . . . . th'.

Commentary: The password of this degree is the one that is the best explained of the three that Craft Masons use. It may, however, be of interest to know that when we learn the origin of these two words, that are alike yet different, it makes even more sense of what we are told. The word that the Hebrews used, 'Sh . . . . . . th', meant, as it sounds, 'a flow of running water', whilst in Arabic the word 'Siblet' still means 'a grain of a cereal'. When these two words are used the failure of one group to aspirate is even better understood.

6th Pause: When the candidate stands at the pedestal but before the Worshipful Master speaks.

Commentary: The ascent of the winding staircase is a most distinctive feature of our English second degree. Its origin was as a means by which the priests could pass between the Holy Place and the three-tiered chambers that were attached to the Temple of Solomon on the North and South sides. Some Second Degree tracing boards correctly show the priests' access to this staircase through the south side wall half-way along the Holy Place. This meant that the priests then ascended from the North side of the next-door room and up the curved stairs to the East. That is why the steps we demonstrate move from North to East. The fifteen or more steps derive from the early Christian tale that Mary, the mother of Jesus, ascended a staircase of fifteen steps to enter the Temple court of the men and was welcomed by a High Priest at the top. One of the Guild Plays performed by some medieval masons portrayed just this event.

7th Pause: When the candidate is kneeling at the Pedestal and just before the Worshipful Master begins the Obligation.

Commentary: When you remember that originally there was but one grade of Mason in a Lodge, that of Fellow or Master of the Craft, you will realise why in our present second degree we lay bare the other arm and foot from that which were referred to in the former degree. In ancient Masonry the candidate was attired as he now is in the third degree. If non-Masons seem puzzled about our dress they forget that working masons roll up their sleeves to work and once had pants that only came to the knee. Stockings were for special days if affordable.

The importance of the square is emphasised as he has his left arm resting in the angle of that implement. In the signs of the degree we see that the same implement is suggested.

8th Pause: When, with the sealing of the obligation over, the Senior Deacon takes the candidate to the right of the Worshipful Master and before the latter speaks.

Commentary: The obligation in this degree is similar to and yet shorter than that in the Entered Apprentice degree. This is because originally there was only one obligation for both grades. The same applies to the Charge as we shall see.

The position of the square and compasses is not only a sign of progress but was originally the only way the two implements were displayed, that is, intertwined. Take a look at the symbols on the nameboards of Past Masters in older lodges and you will note that they show this sign and not that of a Master Mason. This is because the working lodges of operative masons were all made up of Fellows and from them the Wardens who ruled the lodges were chosen. That is why the boards bear what we call the Fellowcraft symbol.

9th Pause: During the passage in which the grip, token and word are given to the newly passed Brother and immediately after the words 'improperly disclose the Secrets entrusted to you'.

Commentary: As we discovered in the Entered Apprentice degree, the secrets are only able to be conveyed when the recipient is standing with a regular step. This is exactly the same in form as in the first degree save that now we have to take two steps before we can be enlightened, thus representing progress in accepted Freemasonry.

The first part of the sign is surely clear but the second needs some explanation. Because we take it with one hand already in place on the left breast we do not appreciate that the Haling Sign here, based on a couple of biblical passages, should really be given by lifting up both hands to the sky as a sign of supplication. Indeed there are some workings of our ritual in which the first part is made, then discharged, and both hands are lifted before the third part is given.

The biblical passage usually referred to is that in which Joshua prayed for the light of day to continue, but there was also another passage in which, while Joshua fought and had his hands full with the battle, Moses prayed for him on a hill nearby and as his arms were weak Aaron and Hur supported them in a raised position so that the Lord might hear his prayer.

10th Pause: At the close of the Worshipful Master's instruction when he says, 'Pass J . . . . n'.

Commentary: The lettering or halving of a 'secret' word was a common practice in the 18th Century or before. It is worth remarking that in some Masonic rituals, especially in the USA, the letters are not given in the order we use but haphazardly, e. g. C. J. A. H. N. I. That really can puzzle the candidate, never mind a Cowan.

The place of the two pillars is often questioned. There should really be no difficulty as the pillars are described as if looking East. In Solomon's Temple that meant looking out of the building whilst with us it means looking in. Facing East, B . . z is on the left and J . . . . n on the right.

The status of J . . . . n as Assistant High Priest is not found in the Volume of the Sacred Law, instead it is recorded in other books of ancient usage (that are called the Pseudepigrapha).

11th Pause: At the end of the interrogation by the Senior Warden as he says, 'Pass J. . . . n'.

Commentary: We thought earlier about the meaning of the words 'Pass B . . z' and now we come to the other half of this admission procedure. That the pillars B . . z and J . . . . n once belonged to one ceremony is made clear by the floor-cloths or early tracing boards which show the pillars together. We know, for example, that in the Grand Lodge of All England at York it was customary up to 1780 to make men Apprentices and Fellows on the same evening. A trace of this practice is still evident in what we have just heard, for the Senior Warden asks, 'And what when conjoined with that in the former degree?'. Clearly the two terms only really make sense when they come together. That is how they were first meant to be. The conjoint meaning is an embellished translation of 1 Kings, chapter 8, verse 13.

12th Pause: After the Senior Warden has invested the new Fellowcraft with his apron and handed him back to the Senior Deacon.

Commentary: Have you ever asked yourself why the Worshipful Master cannot open the Lodge without going through the Junior Warden or close the Lodge himself? Why does he here let the Senior Warden have the privilege of putting the apron on the new Fellowcraft? It is because we are here reverting to the tradition of operative masonry in which a Warden, not a Master Mason, ruled the stonemasons' lodge. In Guild Masonry, in imitation of the way a Guild was ruled, the new idea of having a Right Worshipful Master crept in but the ancient rights of the office of Warden were still preserved.

In earlier times the way to distinguish a Fellow from an Apprentice was to turn down the flap of the white apron and turn up one corner so that it could hold a square. Now we have rosettes which are just the decorated forms of what were old buttonholes.

13th Pause: At the end of the Worshipful Master's remarks on the apron and after saying, '...the wonderful works of the Almighty.'

Commentary: If you wonder why a Craftsman is expected to make the Liberal Arts and Sciences his future study then you need to know that as it was from the Craftsmen that the exclusive group known as Master Masons were selected so to attain that rank you had to be proficient in understanding those seven subjects. For example, you had to know about the stars so as to be able to lay out a site, or to know about musical harmony in order to erect buildings useful for speakers and choirs.

The connection of the Seven Liberal Arts and Sciences with the winding staircase is brought to our attention in the explanation of the Tracing Board. What is interesting is that here we see the natural link between what working stonemasons had to know and what naturally interested the early Free and Accepted Masons.

14th Pause: At the close of the Charge at the south-east corner.

Commentary: This charge, like the obligation, is quite short because it is a second part of what was once a single Apprentice and Fellow whole. The reason why the new Fellowcraft is placed in the south-east corner is to mark his progress from a rough ashlar, that was meant to be between his feet in the north-east, to the smooth ashlar that should be placed here, as it is in many lodges.

The invitation 'to extend your researches into the hidden mysteries of nature and science' echoes the study of the Seven Liberal Arts and Sciences just mentioned with 'the wonderful works of the Almighty'. The symbolic connection of such labour with a true winding staircase is here very striking. If it is a stairway, as in a lighthouse or castle turret, then we cannot see what 'mystery' might be revealed round the next step.

15th Pause: When the Worshipful Master, after the presentation of the tools, says, 'to restore yourself to your personal comforts. '

Commentary: The tools presented in this degree are those of a working stonemason and those which still adorn the seats of the Worshipful Master and his Wardens. It is because we are now Free & Accepted Masons that we do what no working mason would do: we 'apply these tools to our morals'. For a proper understanding of these tools in this sense we need to be aware that there is a longer explanation of them which teaches us important lessons, not least about our duty to God.

However, we should note that, as we have been instructed earlier, even the shorter form of this presentation concludes with the words, 'we hope to ascend to those immortal mansions whence all goodness emanates'. We are not going to hear about the Tracing Board but that also reminds us of God's presence. As the seal of our United Grand Lodge declares, it is not just holiness that is required of us but 'Holiness to the Lord'.

5

Commentary on the Third Degree Ceremony

This presentation of the ceremony starts when the Inner Guard, as if having enquired of the Tyler about the candidate, says he will report to the Worshipful Master. On this occasion the obligation ought to be given in full except for the affirmation and sealing. When there is a dialogue between the Senior Deacon and the Wardens only one of the Wardens need be involved each time. This presentation ends with the explaining of the tools. No one present takes any part in the ceremony except the designated officers and everyone else remains seated throughout. What now follows are the points when there is a Pause whilst an explanation is given of what has just taken place.

1st Pause: When the Worshipful Master has asked the Inner Guard if he can vouch for the candidate and the Inner Guard has said, 'I do, Worshipful Master'.

Commentary: The powerful aid which the candidate here is said to possess consists first, as in the previous degrees, of the 'help of God'. This repeated emphasis on the necessary assistance that only a Supreme Being can provide is surely enough to question the repeated claim that the Craft degrees are simply concerned with encouraging moral endeavour. The awareness of, and reliance on, an active Divine power in our lives is a constant part of what being a Freemason means.

This truth about our Society, the name we were given in the first degree, is underlined by the description of this degree as 'sublime'. This means that we are to be admitted to special experiences of an uplifting nature. We may not reach the goal first intended in this degree, and stated by the Junior Warden in the opening, the genuine secrets, but at least we know that the full circle of God's plan for us is meant to be revealed somewhere that we may attain because we have the help of the compasses and not just the square. The G. A. O. T. U. is calling us to be fellow architects of our destiny as men and as Masons.

2nd Pause: When the Candidate has stood up after prayer.

Commentary: This ceremony begins with a recognition of the Architect and Ruler of the Universe. Yet we do not simply acknowledge our Creator. We seek his 'grace' or divine aid so that we may share 'the mysterious secrets' of a Master Mason. Let us note that there is no mention here of any 'substituted secrets'.

The prayer further seeks divine assistance in passing through the experience of death so that there may be a rising from the 'tomb of transgression'. This may pose a question or two for us since what is described here does not properly fit what we know is to follow. The words speak of a dead person's emergence from a tomb and not a grave, and the tomb moreover of one who had done wrong rather than one to whom wrong was done. Yet no candidates actually die in this ceremony and Hiram is accredited with more significance than he merits. Was this prayer perhaps first compiled for a form of ceremony somewhat different to our present one? On the other hand mention of an 'hour of trial' does fit very well with what is to follow.

3rd Pause: At the end of the third perambulation when the Senior Warden says, 'Pass, T . . . . n'

Commentary: We are so used to having this Password that it may never occur to us to question its relevance to this degree. What do 'the first Artificer in Metals' or 'Worldly Possessions' have to do with what we know takes place later? If one suggests that Hiram Abiff supervised the casting of the pillars, B . . z and J . . . . . n, then surely this Password belongs more fittingly to the first or second degree. It is interesting therefore to discover that in French exposures of this degree from

1743–1751 we read: 'The Password of the Apprentice is T . . . . n, of the second degree is Sh . . . . th and of the third degree G . . . . m'. For those further qualified in Masonry it will be seen that an alteration of words took place later and so a gap appeared in the third degree. Was the password 'T . . . . n' adopted to fill that gap?

Moreover 'Worldly Possessions' also fits the first degree best as a reminder of what we have to surrender as we enter the Craft. These alterations suggest that this degree is not the complete one that once it was.

4th Pause: When the 'proper steps' to the East have been taken and the candidate stands before the pedestal.

Commentary: We perhaps need to be reminded, as was pointed out in the first degree, that the steps for reaching the East are not regular ones although they have some 'proper significance'. What matters is that we recognise that we are passing over a grave in roughly the form of a square and from then on can proceed with renewed confidence.

It may be of interest to learn that in some Lancashire lodges, as no doubt elsewhere, the old custom of having a Brother actually lying in the shroud as the candidate passes over him is still practised. You then learn to lift your legs as you cross where a body lies. After the candidate has moved forward the recumbent Brother removes himself so as to leave the space for the new Master Mason. In other places, such as at Spilsby and Barnstaple, a real cavity in the floor of the lodge is at this point opened up.

5th Pause: At the close of the obligation and before the affirmation with sealing by the lips.

Commentary: As appropriate for so 'sublime' a degree the obligation is both long and detailed. The Deity is addressed as the 'Most High' and the lodge is additionally described as 'duly constituted', suggesting that it was originally created as a separate body from the operative lodge. This is correct historically because, as we learnt earlier, the working site lodge was composed of Fellows and ruled over by a Warden. The Master Mason did not appear in that lodge.

The reference to 'within the length of my Cable-tow' is fully explained in Bernard Jones's Compendium. It may well have meant originally a distance of some 3 miles or as far as a Mason could be expected to walk to lodge. Today it means as far as reasonable circumstances permit. Its original use leads us back into Noachic Masonry, but that is another story.

The most distinctive section of this obligation refers to the F. P. O. F. about which more will be said shortly but this part of our tradition dates from at least the 18th Century or possibly earlier. It may interest you to know that in early French working it was 'cheek to cheek', rather than breast to breast, and in a working in London in the 1730s there were six points of Fellowship because the sixth was the whispering of the word in the ear.

6th Pause: When, the sealing being omitted, the emblems on the Volume of the Sacred Law have been indicated and the Worshipful Master says, 'Rise, newly obligated Master Mason'.

Commentary: Mention was made at the entrance of the candidate for this degree that he came with the aid of the compasses and here he is shown that they are now made available for his use. It is worth pointing out that the compasses were the tool of a working Master Craftsman who was skilled enough to create curved items such as keystones and arches. Here, of course, for Free and Accepted Masons, it means that we can begin to embrace all that Freemasonry has to offer, especially when we shall have discovered the point within a circle in the fully completed Master Mason degree.

7th Pause: After the words in the Exhortation, 'equal to the stain of falsehood and dishonour', have been said.

Commentary: This passage of ritual is, when thoughtfully considered and rendered, one of the highlights of this degree. It consists of a review of the path which the new Master Mason has previously taken. What needs to be again emphasised is that whilst the moral efforts of a Brother are described, the aim and goal of all his doings is 'above all to bend with humility and resignation to the will of the Great Architect' and 'to dedicate one's heart to (God's) glory' as well as 'the welfare of our fellow mortals'.

Even when, in the second degree, our intellectual faculty is engaged, it is to lead us to 'the throne of God himself' and it is to that presence, and with that aid, that we are to face even death. It is here worth remembering that the 'Throne of God' in the Temple of Solomon was the golden plate on the top of the Ark of the Covenant in the Sanctum Sanctorum. That is where Masons are meant finally to discover themselves, as the seal of our Grand Lodge on their certificates suggests.

8th Pause: When the candidate has been lowered to the ground after the Worshipful Master says, '...lifeless at his feet.'

Commentary: The story here told is so familiar that we can be forgiven for not always realizing its significance. Although the Temple of Solomon was not completed the Holy of Holies was finished and set apart at the western end of the Holy Place. What we are told happened here was that since the Holy Place was not yet consecrated for the use of the priests alone Hiram Abiff used to go there at high noon to pray about the work, standing before the door of the Sanctum Sanctorum. It was as he came away from there to the South door leading to the side chambers he was met by the first Fellowcraft who was eager to have the Master's secret. Attacked for his inevitable refusal, he goes to the North door and is similarly treated. It is then, turning to the East door, that was the porchway or entrance, that he is fatally struck and dies.

What this meant was that in a strange way the ancient building tradition that required a sacrifice at the threshold of all new buildings was provided. It also meant that Solomon had indeed to ensure the proper consecration of the Temple to cleanse it of the stain of this 'heinous crime'. What the real secret was that Hiram Abiff refused to give will be discussed soon.

9th Pause: When, having assisted with the raising, the Wardens are invited to 'resume your seats'.

Commentary: In his remarks before the attempts made to raise the Brother representing Hiram Abiff the Worshipful Master spoke of Hiram's 'unshaken fidelity to the sacred trust reposed in him'. This was a reference to his repeated unwillingness to share with the three Fellowcrafts a secret restricted to the Master Masons. Strictly we should say that he refused to give up his part of the secret because it was a secret that had to be shared by three participants to make it complete. Whilst it was right that this true secret was temporarily lost by his death it was not lost altogether for when another suitable Mason was appointed in his place, as did in fact take place, the secret was restored.

The greatest operative secret of the medieval Master Masons was the knowledge of how to create a right angled triangle by a 3:4:5 formula. That is why in some ancient Masonry the rulers of a Guild lodge had rods of 18in, 24in and 30in. One such 18in rule dated 1663 is still in existence in York.

The secret of Accepted Freemasonry was a tripartite Word or Name. Its discovery was originally the climax of this degree. Indeed, third degree tracing boards in Holland still display the Name but do not explain it. For us the completed secret now has to be found elsewhere.

10th Pause: At the end of the Charge that now follows and when the Worshipful Master says, '. . the faithful and obedient of the human race'.

Commentary: The charge which has just been delivered is the other highlight of this degree. Its message is sublime as would befit the complete Master Mason degree. It rightly reminds us that our only real hope of facing the future beyond death lies in the light of divine guidance, the emphasis once again being on how dependent on God's assistance we need to be.

What is surprising is that it is only at this stage of our Masonic progress, with the immediate prospect of the grave and of our mortal remains, that our thoughts are supposed to be led to that ancient study, The Knowledge of Oneself. In several European workings this comes at a much earlier stage because it is so crucial for our balanced and sensible behaviour towards others.

Surprising also, in what is nowadays supposed to be a de-Christianised Freemasonry, are the references to 'The Lord of Life' who will enable us to conquer evil, and that 'Bright morning star' (a clear reference to Christ in the Bible's Book of Revelation) 'whose rising', which here means resurrection, 'brings peace and salvation to the faithful…' we have here a real reflection of 18th Century English Freemasonry.

11th Pause: When the Worshipful Master invites the candidate to retire to restore his personal comforts and says, '…the Ss, T. and W. will be further explained'.

Commentary: You will have noticed that following the Charge the Worshipful Master swings the new Master Mason from north to south. Why does he do that? The answer is that as was explained in the Exhortation this Brother, like all of us, has passed from the first degree, represented by the north-east corner, to the second degree in the south-east corner. It is from this latter spot that he appropriately takes his third regular step, in which alone he can receive the present 'secrets'. What is not indicated at this stage is that these signs are 'substituted ones' though we shall learn that very shortly. It is true, as the Worshipful Master says later, that these will 'designate you Master Masons throughout the Universe' but only 'until time and circumstances shall [note shall and not may] restore the genuine ones'. It is important for us to realise that these are temporary, makeshift alternatives to real ones that have existed from Time Immemorial and can be discovered.

In the F. P. O. F. we need to note that 'knee to knee' is a reminder of daily prayer in which we remember others' needs and that 'hand over back' in earlier practice meant hand into back so that it truly represented a support for another's character in their absence.

The Word that is given turns out to be two words. This is because at the union of the Moderns and Antients Grand Lodges they could not agree on which of their substituted Words to use and with good English compromise they agreed to use both.

12th Pause: When the Worshipful Master has commented on the apron and says, '...the Brethren in the inferior degrees'.

Commentary: You will notice that though we are now in the new context of a Master Mason's lodge, the right of the Warden to put the apron on a newly raised Brother is still recognised. This is so striking that it suggests three things.

One is that perhaps there had been occasions in a Guild lodge when a Master Mason was so recognised. Secondly, that perhaps the present Master Mason is really only a glorified Fellow or Master craftsman because he is without the true secret, and is therefore still under a Warden's rule. That would explain why Master Masons in a lodge opened in their degree are asked to leave when at an Installation. It is because they are not true Master Masons. Or thirdly, because the United Grand Lodge wanted to retain a certain similarity of pattern in the manner of investing all Brethren even if it did break tradition. Further, it is still a matter for research to discover what are, or were, 'those great duties you have just solemnly engaged yourself to observe'.

13th Pause: At the end of the extended History when the Worshipful Master has said, '...the heinousness of their crimes so amply merited'.

Commentary: It hardly needs stressing that the dramatic tale just recounted is one of the wholly fictitious sections of speculative Freemasonry. We know from the Volume of the Sacred Law that figures like Solomon, Hiram of Tyre and even Hiram Abiff and Adoniram existed and played parts in some measure comparable to what our ritual describes. There were also officers of the working masons called Menatschim or Overseers and being human they were no doubt as susceptible to greed, envy and anger as we are. Yet whether the events just described took place is totally unproven by any known evidence. It is a good and even a moral tale but we can claim nothing more for it.

In the course of the story Solomon informs the returning craftsmen that 'by his untimely death the secrets of a Master Mason are lost'. As explained above, we need to realise that he means 'temporarily lost' and the resulting 'substituted secrets' were also meant to be temporary and for Craftsmen only. Perhaps we have here the solution of the puzzle that was raised over the investiture of a Master Mason by a Warden.

14th Pause: At the end of the Tracing Board explanation.

Commentary: The explanation of the Tracing Board in this degree is one of the most unsatisfactory parts of the whole ceremony. Between 1730 and 1760 there are many descriptions of how Solomon insisted that his chief artist be buried in the Holy of Holies itself. Yet in our present version, bearing in mind Jewish law and custom, such a possibility appears quite unacceptable. We are still told, however, that he was buried as near to this spot as was possible. What does that mean? Could it be that as the Temple was not completed and hence unconsecrated Hiram was carried into the area which became the Holy of Holies and was buried beneath it. Some rituals say this and that it was in a vault that was uncovered later.

Again, when the Dormer is said to give 'light to the same' we should realise that it was the Porch of that place that is meant to be lit up. It could not be the Sanctum Sanctorum as that was, we know, always in total darkness.

We are also told nothing about the old cipher writing on the coffin or why the veils of the Holy Place are drawn back. That needs more explanation than can be given here.

15th Pause: At the end of showing the alternate signs.

Commentary: The signs as English Freemasons give them are mainly self-explanatory though the interpretations of the sign of Joy and Exultation vary considerably. The most satisfactory form would seem to be to join the hands over the head in a nearly triangular manner, thus representing the way the wings of the Cherubim appear over the Ark of the Covenant. This should also be the Grand or Royal sign. There should be no clapping of hands because the Temple was a silent place both during and after building.

The sign of Grief and Distress as used in North America seems, from my acquaintance with it, to be given by dropping the bent arms in three positions parallel with the neck, the chest and the stomach thus relating them to the three penal areas. The founder of the Mormon religion was a Mason and he gave a sign just like this when he appealed to Masons outside to be released from the gaol at Albany.

16th Pause: When the tools of a Master Mason have been presented.

Commentary: At the outset of these Commentaries mention was made of the Great Architect's desire that Master Masons should also become good architects. The implements just explained are those of that profession because that is what medieval Master Masons were. The skirret, so named after an old Scandinavian word, 'skirra' meaning 'to whirr like a thread leaving a spindle', was used for marking out a new building site. The various forms of marking and registering plans for the building are represented by the pencil, and the compasses were the most advanced instrument available for both designing and creating beautiful items with which to decorate the structure.

What is most noticeable as we come to moralise on these tools is that we are again called to consider the dimensions of divinity. The Volume of the Sacred Law, our words recorded by the Almighty Architect and the commands or justice of our divine Creator are all specifically mentioned. Is it not very telling that as we come into this degree with God's aid we come to its close with the hope of ascending to the Grand Lodge above where the world's Great Architect lives and rules for ever? Master Masons and Craftsmen are always to have God in view.

6

Commentary on the Installation Ceremony (except Board of Installed Masters)

This commentary is particularly intended to assist those who are to rehearse the ceremony of Installation prior to their own or another's entry to the Chair, but also to provide an alternative item that might be offered as a presentation to an Installed Masters lodge in place of the usual lecture. In order to keep the occasion within a reasonable time span it is suggested that if this is for a Lodge of Installed Masters it is declared that the lodge is open in the first and second degrees, but if in a demonstration then we open in the First Degree and declare it open in the Second. The Obligation need only have the first and last phrases and in the Investiture of officers there is no need for the extended wordings. The Commentary ends before the delivery of the three addresses to the Worshipful Master, Wardens and Brethren. In what follows the various pauses indicate when each Commentary should be given and after the Commentary work resumes without further notice.

1st Pause: When the Installing Master has resumed the lodge, or has declared it to be, in the Second Degree.

Commentary: The antiquity of what we are now about to do is revealed at once by our starting the Installation ceremony in the Fellowcraft degree. This transports us back to the days of operative stonemasonry when a working site lodge consisted only of fellows or craftsmen who chose one of their number to be the Warden ruling over them. In those days no Master Mason was allowed, or expected, to share in the affairs of the lodge and you may notice that all that now takes place, even though the title 'Master' is used, is done in the Second degree. It is also to be noted that as apprentices were not originally part of any lodge they are still excluded even though they now exercise a right to vote for the new ruler of the lodge. In the USA it is still the case that in some lodges voting is restricted to Master Masons.

2nd Pause: When the Past Master presenting the Brother for the Chair has said, 'receive at your hands the benefit of Installation'.

Commentary: The recognition of the next ruler of the lodge by his predecessors is an essential element in the ongoing wellbeing of the lodge and that is why this presentation has its place. The form of the presentation may vary for in some cases two Past Masters do the presentation, sometimes it is Brethren especially known to the Master-elect and sometimes it is the Director of Ceremonies, if he is a Past Master. What is being signalled here is that the Master-elect is a worthy successor to those who have preceded him and is so presented by those who have shared the responsibility which he is now to undertake. It is worth noting that the ceremony of Installation is here described as a benefit. This does not imply that there are future advantages accruing to a ruler but simply that to be correctly placed in the Chair is an act that is 'well done': benefit.

3rd Pause: When the Installed Master has said to the Brethren, 'to qualify him for the discharge of the duties of his important trust'.

Commentary: The words addressed to the brethren by the Installing Master are so familiar that it is easy to overlook their actual meaning. The 'established Custom' to which he refers is that every year there will be selected 'an experienced Craftsman to preside over them in the capacity of Master'. This reflects again the ancient operative system even if our requirement is that such a craftsman must have been a Warden already. The continuing tradition is that only Wardens can be rulers of a lodge. This is emphasised by the word for this ex-Warden's next task: to preside 'in the capacity' of Master. This is not, apparently, to be a new grade or degree but simply a new function as the officer ruling over whoever may be members of the lodge. As a further assurance of the suitability and acceptability of the chosen Craftsman he is to be presented to a Board of Installed Masters, 'the better to qualify him' for his forthcoming duties. Further comment will soon be made about this 'Board' but it needs to be noted that it is only in their presence that the Installation can now take place. If it is not a new grade it is at least a new step.

4th Pause: After the Installing Master, addressing the Master-elect, asks: '...on these qualifications?'.

Commentary: It is interesting that the first qualification is one that speaks of his having been highly esteemed among 'his brethren and Fellows' as if the Masons over whom he is to rule are the Craftsmen and Apprentices. This would accord with the tradition which has already been amply illustrated.

The next qualification now introduces a new note because the Master-elect must also have been 'raised'. This is something that we may take for granted but we need to be reminded that entering the 'Master Mason' degree was throughout the 18th Century an optional extra for most Freemasons and therefore it could not always be assumed that a Brother who was an ex-Warden Craftsman had taken that step. What exactly 'having been raised' meant we shall come to in the next commentary.

In both the second and third qualifications it is noticeable that 'skill in the Noble Science' and 'Ancient Charges, Regulations and Landmarks' is meant to be actually the case. Is it fair to ask when we last looked at the really Ancient Charges or made ourselves familiar with the Landmarks?

5th Pause: When the Installing Master has requested all below the 'rank of an Installed Master to retire'.

Commentary: We have now to understand what is a crucial part of the proceedings. The point of 'raising' is to introduce a Freemason to what will be the eventual culmination of his Masonic journey. He is now to learn that there are areas which only those with further knowledge as a Master

Mason do attain. It is, of course, nowadays generally understood that the ceremony of Installation is neither a degree nor does it confer any further Masonic distinction than that of being recognised as the ostensible ruler of the lodge. If this is so then one must assume that it is a further part of the Master Mason degree in which it is held. This would appear to be confirmed by the fact that those not yet entitled to share in this section of the third degree are required to leave what is a lodge open in a degree that they are supposed to have already completed. It needs recalling that in the 18th Century there were many lodges that regarded what now followed as the degree of Excellent Mason or Passed Master and it is from such lodges that there descended the fuller Inner Working that we cannot speak of here. The body that now meets is called a Board because it was originally the qualified brethren left at the table or board when the rest of the brethren had departed. (See the note on p.51).

6th Pause: When the Installing Master has made the first proclamation and says, 'I call on you to greet him as Master Masons ... taking the time from me (or the Director of Ceremonies)'.

Commentary: It is noteworthy that even when the Board of Installed Masters is closed we are still in the third degree and hence the other Master Masons may be re-admitted. Interestingly, though they are those who left the lodge in this degree prior to the Installation they still have to make a perambulation showing the sign of a Master Mason as the proper salute to the new ruler. This can be the occasion when we are reminded that the penal signs of the three degrees were once described, by where the hands were placed, as Guttural (at the throat), Pectoral (at the breast) and Ventral or Umbilical (at the navel). The use of such signs as a form of salute not only reminded Brethren of their past obligations but was a reassurance to the new Master of the members' allegiance.

7th Pause: When the Entered Apprentice tools have been presented and the Brethren have been invited to take their places.

Commentary: The proclamation that has now been made three times in open lodge was introduced in order that those who were not permitted to share in the actual Installation or, as was more and more the case, excluded from the lodge room during this ceremony, should now be aware that what was required had taken place in due form. In Bristol each proclamation is preceded by a trumpet fanfare whilst lodges elsewhere have something similar played on an organ. What is also intended is that the news shall be made known not only in each degree but at morning, noon and night.

8th Pause: When the Installed Master has made presentations to the Worshipful Master and says, '...the Brethren may not plead ignorance of them'.

Commentary: Because the first Warrant of Constitution of the lodge was presented by a representative of the Grand Master, with the recipient standing out of respect, it is now customary for the Worshipful Master to be standing as the Warrant is again presented to him. It should be noted, however, that there are some very old lodges in which the Worshipful Master does not stand at this point and that is because the lodge over which he is now to preside either never had a Warrant so presented originally or was inaugurated without a Warrant at all. In these cases the fact that re-presenting a Warrant is now part of the accepted Masonic practice does not require anything other than happens with the succeeding items at this point. If one sits for them, as one does, then the same posture is thought adequate. It is not for those from outside such a lodge to comment.

An up-to-date copy of the Book of Constitutions is what is now the next thing to be handed to the Worshipful Master. It is not sufficient to say that as the Worshipful Master will have received a copy of these regulations when he was made a Mason he is adequately provided for. The constant changes in a Book of Constitutions demand that what the new Worshipful Master is to possess must be the version that is currently authorised if he is to 'set the lodge right'.

It is equally necessary that the bye-laws of the lodge that he is given should be those that are presently in force. The previous requirement that the bye-laws should be read to the members once in each year was a tradition from the days when there might be members who could not read them for themselves. It is now recognised that as all the members are literate such a requirement is no longer appropriate. This does not mean that all members will have read them and it will not be unfitting that a reminder to read them should be part of a Master's instruction.

9th Pause: When the new Junior Warden has been conducted to his seat.

Commentary: The appointment of the two Wardens is a timely reminder of our Accepted Masonic origins. As was stated early in this commentary a working site lodge of stonemasons was, as in most operative trade bodies, ruled over by a Warden chosen from the craftsmen. It is still noticeable that it is only as the Senior Warden is invested that it says, 'the insignia of your office', thus marking his peculiar position. Later, as guilds were chartered, there appeared new officers, based on the pattern of local government, itself derived from church practice. Thus, instead of a Rector and two wardens there was a Master, addressed as Right Worshipful like a Mayor, and two wardens. These were at first simply the officers of the Guild Court but eventually they became the appointed officers of a Lodge.

In 18th century Masonry, the Wardens took up their places for the admission or conducting of a candidate beside the two pillars that were first drawn and then modelled as lodge furniture. Hence the phrase, 'the column of your office', and the post-Union practice of having miniature columns on their pedestals. The gavel was likewise a replacement of what had been the wands, then batons, that the Worshipful Master and these officers once used. What happened to those wands we shall see shortly. It is worth remarking that the gavels are given, as with a Worshipful Master, for keeping order in the lodge and not, as too often seems the case, for disturbing the lodge with every item of business. If the brethren are orderly then the gavel should not be needed.

It has also to be noted that the Senior Warden is charged to close 'after having seen that every Brother has had his due'. These old words remind us that in a working lodge it was the Warden who paid the craftsmen their due wages. It is this ancient duty that is now recalled every time the lodge closes and in some lodges the Senior Warden replies to the Worshipful Master's query as to whether the wages have been paid, 'They have, Worshipful Master, to the best of my knowledge and belief'.

In the case of the Junior Warden, he is charged to inform the Brethren, at what was once a central table, when they should cease from their ritual activities and engage in dining and conversation. It is worth our noting that as there was then no Director of Ceremonies the Worshipful Master did not have anyone to tell him what to do. One wonders why they ever began to do so at the festive board. Is it because there has not been sufficient understanding of the ritual? Or not enough training in a Worshipful Master's duties?

The jewels worn by the Wardens need no further explanation as they are amply commented on by the Worshipful Master.

10th Pause: When the Treasurer is seated after investiture.

Commentary: Though it is now assumed that there will always be a lodge Chaplain and Treasurer it has to be recorded that these were not offices in all lodges from the beginning. The appointment of a clergyman depended on who was suitable or locally available and that is why, to this day, there are some Masters of lodges who recite the prayers at the opening and closing of the lodge even though there is now some brother designated as Chaplain. The Worshipful Master is doing what was probably normal in that lodge until the office of Chaplain was an authorised appointment after the 1813 Union.

The post of Treasurer was very similar. It is known that in many old lodges it was customary for the lodge's money to be the responsibility of the Master and Wardens and that is why the lodge chest had three keyholes. It was so that it could not be opened without the attendance of the three officers. It was again at the Union that the occasional office of a Treasurer in some lodges was now deemed to be more proper for each lodge. It was from this period that the idea of accounts being presented and approved arose. You should note that the Treasurer now has just one key and must have the confidence and so the vote of all the members.

11th Pause: After the appointment of a Director of Ceremonies.

Commentary: It might well be thought that the Secretary ought also to be voted for as one who has the approval of all the Brethren. In some lodges in the 18th Century it was the case that all the officers, though far fewer in number, were voted for by the full lodge members and to this day there are many lodges, especially in the North of England, that are called on for a handclap by the members when an officer is newly seated. It may seem to visitors an odd thing to do but it is in fact the residue of the days when this was the sign of approval by the lodge members. Now it seems more like congratulation.

The post of Director of Ceremonies needs a little more comment. Before the union of the two Grand Lodges there was no need for such an officer because the Worshipful Master was expected 'to rule and govern his lodge'. After the Union the Worshipful Master and his Wardens were now expected to stay in their seats and hence could not control those on the floor as they had done previously. A new post, that of Director of Ceremonies, was created and he was given the Worshipful Master's wand of office to signify that he was acting for and with some of the delegated power of the Master. As a further indication of this it is interesting to learn that as in medieval times the rector of a parish bore a staff with a cross at its head so the Director of Ceremony's wand, or baton, today has just such crossed symbols.

12th Pause: When the new Junior Deacon has been conducted to his seat.

Commentary: The deacons acting in a ceremonial role was another innovation after the 1813 Union. Previously, such deacons as are mentioned in Antients' lodges were those who passed round the table to take discreet messages from the Master to his Wardens. That is why that is still the description given of their task when they are questioned at the

Lodge Opening. It is only when they are invested in the post-Union form of the Installation ceremony that any mention is made of their attendance on candidates. This was now necessary because, as was mentioned earlier, the Master and Wardens after the Union were expected to remain in their seats and so their previous involvement on the floor in the ceremonies now needed to be undertaken by others. That is why the Wardens' wands were now made the Deacons' sign of office.

The symbol on the top of the wands has changed from time to time as variations in different lodges makes clear. In some Durham Province lodges the symbol is a crescent moon for the Senior Deacon and a sun for the Junior. This plainly demonstrates that the Deacons had wands related to the Senior and Junior Wardens. In some late 18th Century lodges a winged Mercury was preferred as a classical reference to a noted messenger. The dove, with hints of ancient Noachic elements in English Freemasonry, was recommended and widely adopted after the Union. As a form of celestial messenger bearing the olive branch of peace and tranquillity it was appropriate after the major Masonic disagreements had been settled.

13th Pause: After the Assistant Secretary is appointed and the words '...two pens in saltire' are said.

Commentary: All the officers mentioned in this section came about as a result of post-Union agreement. Assistants to the Secretary and Director of Ceremonies and Organists are hardly ever mentioned in the 18th century and are a sign of the desire by the United Grand Lodge to organise the Craft more efficiently. This is equally the case with the post of Almoner. There had been a concern for the welfare of members and their dependents, as well as caring for the poor and destitute, from the earliest times but it was inclined to be haphazard and intermittent and this officer could now regularly inform the members of, and request from them, the help needed. The same can be said of the much newer office of Charity Steward since he can relieve the Almoner of money-raising whilst also keeping the lodge informed of common charity projects.

14th Pause: After the invested Stewards have returned to their places.

Commentary: The posts of Inner Guard and Stewards were also post-Union innovations. In the 18th Century and previously the job of attending the inner door of the lodge was shared between the Junior Warden and the newest initiate. The Warden responded to all knocks on the door except those of the candidate, for whose entry his last predecessor was present. Armed first with a trowel and then later with a dagger or poignard it was one new Mason who pricked the flesh of the next. When the Wardens were limited in their movements it was decided to have a permanent officer at the inner door and hence the post of Inner Guard was created. It should be noted that such is the power of tradition that when there is a knock on the door the Worshipful Master still goes through the old doorkeeper, the Junior Warden.

Stewards were known in some pre-Union Moderns lodges and performed similar duties to the Antients' deacons. Since the post of Deacon was now newly settled and the time of 'refreshment' was after the ceremonial work was ended, the office of Steward became attached to the festive board. This had been the ancient tradition of the Grand Stewards in the Premier Grand Lodge. In lodges where there is no waitress service they can still be very actively involved.

15th Pause: When the Tyler has been invested and withdraws.

Commentary: This is one of the oldest and most honoured of Masonic posts. When Freemasons met in taverns and inns, even if in a room on an upper floor, there was clearly a need for this private meeting to be kept secure, quite apart from the task of receiving and preparing candidates for admission. The Tyler was also often the deliverer of the lodge summons and it was partly for this reason that he was provided with an overcoat, examples of which are still extant in some Masonic museums. Another reason was that he often sat on a draughty landing if no preparation room was provided. The Tyler's farewell toast obviously fitted well as the closing act of a separate festive board.

7

Commentary on the Mark Degree(s)

As with all the other commentaries in this book this one is first and foremost intended as an alternative to a straightforward rehearsal of the Mark Degree in a so-called Lodge of Instruction. It could, however, be used in a regular meeting of a Mark lodge when no candidate is in attendance and when there might otherwise be a rehearsal or a lecture. As will be noted, to offset the time needed for the comments, a number of shortenings in the usual ritual are suggested but they can be varied according to each lodge's wishes. The purpose of this exercise is to enable Mark Master Masons to increase their understanding of, and hence their interest in, the ancient degree that they now practice. The presentation, as elsewhere, requires only the participation of the team involved. All other persons present remain seated throughout.

1st Pause: When the Tyler has communicated the Pass grip and word to the Inner Guard.

Commentary: The close link between the Craft and Mark ceremonies suggested by the ritual is a result of the traditional association of these parts of ancient Freemasonry. What may at first surprise us is that though anyone who seeks the Mark Master degree is required to have been already raised as a Master Mason the candidate is here reported as being a Fellowcraft. One reason for this arrangement is that in fact the degree of Mark Master Mason as we now have it is composed of two older and separate degrees of which more will be said shortly. The other reason is that, as we have just heard, the status of a Mark Master Mason enables a Brother to 'preside over a Lodge of Operative Masons'. We know that such a lodge was composed only of Fellows and it was from them that they chose one to rule as Warden. As is the case even with an Accepted Craft lodge those who are to be rulers have first to be recognised and obligated in a Second Degree lodge.

2nd Pause: When the Worshipful Master has approved the Password and grip and the Inner Guard has returned to the West.

Commentary: It may be noted that personal belief in a Supreme Being, here referred to as The Great Overseer of the Universe, is still an initial requirement of all Mark Master Masons as it is of all Craft brethren. The distinctive grip and word have their own special relevance to the story of the Mark as related later.

3rd Pause: When the candidate has been properly admitted by the Inner Guard and stands to the left of the Senior Warden.

Commentary: The candidate is reminded of the tools which were employed to 'impress' him on his entry to other degrees and is then struck with the Mallet and Chisel. It is worth recalling that these implements were first presented to us as part of the working tools of the First Degree, though the ancient English maul or mallet was replaced by the more modern gavel. Unlike as in the First Degree, however, the uses of the mallet and chisel here are not allegorised but are intended to have their practical use understood. As they indent the stone with significant marks so they are used now to remind the candidate that entry into Mark Masonry is a significant step.

4th Pause: When the Worshipful Master invited the candidate to rise after prayer.

Commentary: We spoke earlier of the requirement of those who sought this degree being Master Masons. In time honoured fashion this qualification is confirmed by the exchanging of the previous degree tokens with the Wardens and Worshipful Master during a perambulation of the lodge room. It is always worth reminding ourselves that a perambulation is of ancient usage since the First Accepted Masons met around a table in the centre of the room.

The Worshipful Master now calls on the candidate to share in an act of prayer thus underlining his declaration that he sought the benefit of this degree 'with the help of God'. The content of the prayer is perhaps too often overlooked as it is delivered swiftly and briefly. It reminds us that those who laboured in this degree were abroad in Lebanon as well as in Israel and that whilst some were engaged in felling cedars or preparing the roughest stone there were others who were privileged to 'put in the Keystone of a mystic arch'. This last employment is, in our English rite never again referred to. Its mention here is a legacy of the Mark's original setting between the Craft and Royal Arch segments of Freemasonry.

5th Pause: When the candidate has chosen his mark and the Worshipful Master says, 'Let me see it.'

Commentary: We have now reached that part of the ceremony where, as was hinted at above, we have the traces of two degrees in what is now treated as one. Moreover we can now see why the candidate arrives as a Fellowcraft. It is because there was originally a degree of Mark Man in which a Fellowcraft chose a mark that would be approved by the Overseer so as to back up his claim for the wages due to him for work done. A Fellowcraft was even meant to be taught a different manner of applying for his wages but we here learn that our candidate was not so instructed. He is therefore taken to the Registrar of Marks to choose a mark that is unique to him in that lodge. It is that mark that the Worshipful Master asks to see that he might check it.

6th Pause: After the Senior Warden says, 'Use it as not abusing it and go on your way rejoicing'.

Commentary: The exchange which has now taken place ought to remind us of one of the distinctive features that the Mark degree has preserved for

Masonry generally. In his traditional role as the ruler of an operative lodge the Senior Warden has the duty and responsibility of paying the craftsmen for their daily labour. It is this same tradition which is still hinted at in the closing of a Craft lodge when the Senior Warden's reply to the Worshipful Master's enquiry about his place includes the words, 'after having seen that every Brother has had his due'. Many lodges then have the Worshipful Master ask, 'And has every Brother had his due?' to which the Senior Warden replies, 'He has, Worshipful Master, to the best of my knowledge and belief.' Here in the Mark the actual setting of those words is revealed. What is more we see here the significance of the Craft term, 'every brother', because the Senior Warden is here acknowledging the sign-manual of a Mark Man whilst later he is to reward those in a higher grade.

7th Pause: When the Senior Deacon has instructed the candidate how to approach the pedestal and has said, 'I will go though them and you will copy me'.

Commentary: We now have a clear declaration that the candidate has been admitted into one of the older Mark degrees and is thus qualified to advance to the next stage. What is to be noted is that it is only when a brother becomes a Mark Master Mason that he is entitled to rule over a lodge, in this case of operative masons. This is what we recognise in the Craft Installation ceremony, that a complete Master Mason is one who has passed through the Chair of a lodge.

The Mark Mason will be fully familiar with the various methods of approaching the East that he will have encountered in passing through the Craft degrees. We notice here that the steps are said to be a combination of those in the Apprentice and Fellowcraft degrees albeit they are in the reverse order and amount to a different total. We are reminded that if the candidate has reached the new status of a Mark Man he is, in relation to the Craft, still a Fellowcraft, which is why the steps are as they are.

8th Pause: After the obligation has been taken and the Worshipful Master has directed the candidate to 're-enter the lodge as a Mark Man'.

Commentary: In assuming the position in which he is to take a further obligation we note that the candidate adopts the pose of a Master Mason. Very similar at first as the words of the obligation may appear there are eventually those slight variations that distinguish Mark ritual from that of the Craft. In particular, of course, there is here mention of a 'mark' that is not simply distinctive of its owner but important in dealing with one's Brethren. The obligation refers, of course, not only to the mark already chosen but to those signs and tokens that are still to be explained. It is also to be noted that there is no restriction on mentioning the penalties as is the current situation in the Craft.

It was at this point that the candidate would once have been seated and invited to listen to a catechism about the lessons of the degree. Today it is acted out by the candidate and others which is why he is told how to re-enter the lodge.

9th Pause: When, following the last decision by the Master Overseer the Worshipful Master says, 'Your work is rejected'.

Commentary: There are three points to be mentioned about the examination process that has just taken place. The first point to note is that not all English Mark lodges carry out this part of the ceremony in the same way. Whilst some lodges have the Deacons and candidate presenting their stones at the same time there are other lodges that have the Deacons first presenting their stones to the Overseers and the candidate is then introduced on his own. These variations illustrate the fact that before 1851 there were lodges working the Mark degrees in their own way and this is one example of such differences. Whilst all new Mark Lodges should follow the current ritual it is to be hoped that these older variations will be retained as reminders of the Mark's ancient past.

The second point to note is that when approved by the Overseers each stone was given a second mark showing that it had received their approval. A third mark might also be made if the master mason wished to indicate some special place for a stone. These latter marks were often hidden when the stones were built into the edifice.

The third point to be made is that if the throwing over of the stone seems harsh it was a distinctly milder treatment than the original practice of throwing the incompetent mason over a precipice or steep place. This was later commuted to carrying the offending stone away as a dead person on a bier before heaving it over and then fining its creator. In earlier Mark ceremonies the stone was lost and the candidate had to return to the quarries to make another.

10th Pause: When the brethren, having paraded for their wages, appear to have an impostor among them and the candidate is allowed to be brought to the Worshipful Master.

Commentary: As was mentioned earlier the Senior Warden was the dispenser of wages and the candidate now learns how this procedure is conducted. He may be surprised at an introduction of music at this point but most Mark Masons would be equally surprised at how much music would already have been heard in Mark lodges, in the North and Midlands especially, where as many as nine or twelve chants are part of the ritual. The great reduction of music in lodge and at the festive board is one of the major changes in Freemasonry over the years.

As the five verses here appointed for the Anthem to be sung in procession are generally reduced to two it is not surprising that Mark Master Masons are unaware of what they might learn if all the verses were used or read in private. One verse speaks of those 'who have passed the square', but not the square and compasses, and 'each have his mark in view'. How many of us in fact have our recorded mark with us as we proceed so as to be able to show it with the sign?

Another verse speaks of Hiram sending to Solomon 'our great Keystone' on which 'appears the name which raises high the fame of all to whom the same is truly known'. Here is a hint of matters beyond the Mark connected with a sacred name and this is further emphasised by the words in the last verse 'to the praiseworthy three who founded this degree'. It may not suit us now to use all the verses of this appointed piece but if we are to appreciate the full measure of this degree we need sometimes to reflect on what its designers intended.

It is now that the distinction of a Mark Man and a Mark Master becomes plain. The candidate presents his hand as previously instructed. He does not know that there is any other manner than that of Mark Man but he soon realises that the penalty of a recent obligation could be a reality. It is only his conductor's pleading that works to his benefit.

11th Pause: When, after making enquiry, the Worshipful Master says, 'Brother Junior Warden resume your seat'.

Commentary: The Worshipful Master, having established that the candidate is only a Mark Craftsman, note the term, and not a Mark Master, allows that ignorance accounts for the mistake and therefore the solution lies in a return to the quarries in order to make a masterpiece. Whilst this decision accords with the ancient practice in the degree it may well cause a sense of confusion in a candidate's mind since he earlier presented proof of his ability. In early forms of the degree, the candidate found and presented work done by another. Hence the idea of an imposter.

What ought also to be reflected on here is the sense of rejection that the candidate has undergone. Herein lies one of the distinctive traits of Mark Masonry, the lesson which we might all learn with advantage in life, that however hard we may labour there is no guarantee that our efforts will be rewarded as we might expect. Humility in the face of such lack of recognition is a hard experience to bear but a Mark Mason is here reminded of this need.

12th Pause: When, after enquiring why work is at a standstill, the Worshipful Master says, 'Richly rewarded shall he be who succeeds in discovering it'.

Commentary: The building work necessary for the completion of the Temple at Jerusalem is now declared to be held up because of the absence of a particular stone. That stone was the key cape-stone of the arch that spanned the doorway into the Holy of Holies at the West end of the inner temple. It was thus not only an important binding stone for the construction of this arch but it was the stone that finally permitted this holiest of Jewish places to be sealed and sanctified when the Temple came to be consecrated by King Solomon. It is therefore only fitting that in our Mark dramatic presentation the Worshipful Master should express such anxiety over the stone's absence since it is, as he says, 'the most important stone in the building'.

It is here that our current presentation of the Mark story again diverges from the older versions. Originally the stone was presented to the Worshipful Master by the skilful craftsman who had, at his command, been despatched to the quarries to prepare some further item that would justify the workman's being recognised as a Mark Master Mason. Here that older sequence is ignored and after inquiry of the overseers it is proposed that the discarded keystone be discovered among the rubbish. The anticipated reward depends upon its safe recovery not its new fashioning.

13th Pause: After the first rewarding of the candidate when the Worshipful Master says, 'and by this sign which is called a lewis'.

Commentary: The stone is found but not, as the Worshipful Master required, and as used to be the case, after 'diligent search'. The former lesson of delving amongst the debris to discover the precious object is no longer felt to be important and hence something of the full value of what had been lost is reduced. To our forebears the search fitted in with the whole purpose of Freemasonry which is throughout a search for those essential elements that together lead us to ultimate truth. It is the searching and finding that make the whole exercise worthwhile. After all the first knocks on the door of a Craft lodge signified 'Seek and ye shall find'.

It is noticeable that to take the fourth regular step in Freemasonry the candidate includes those of all the previous degrees. The signs and tokens to which he is now entitled include those given at his entrance and obligation, and these with others are now explained by the use of the Volume of the Sacred Law. The ingenuity of the ritual formers in so devising the grips and passwords from the story of how materials were transported to the Holy City merits our admiration as well as assisting our remembering of their use. The introduction of the 'lewis' is particularly telling. The full significance of this term is found in my book, 'The Arch and the Rainbow'.

14th Pause: After the communication of the Mark Master Mason signs and words and their testing by the Junior and Senior Wardens when the Senior Warden has said, 'Pass K . . . . . th and M . . k W . . l'.

Commentary: It will be noted that passages from the Volume of the Sacred Law are again used to assist the understanding of the various signs that are now communicated. As mentioned earlier there are some lodges in which these texts are set to music rather than just read but the important thing is that however they are rendered their meaning should be grasped. Poor singing is as unhelpful as inattentive listening.

Twice this command 'to hear with thine ears' is given to the new Mark Master Mason and in nothing that is heard is this more important than when we hear in Psalm 118 verse 22, 'The stone which the builders refused is become the head stone of the corner'. The immediate relevance of these words to what has happened to the candidate is clear even though there may be a moment's question as to why what was for him a keystone is here spoken of as 'the headstone of the corner'. The message that is here meant to be conveyed is that just as the first and chief corner stone was that which a Mason represented when he was made an Apprentice so, having advanced in knowledge and experience, the stone that he now represents has become a similar feature of key importance. The imagery changes but the truth remains the same. Good workmanship will, at last, be acknowledged.

15th Pause: After the new Mark Master Mason has been invested with apron and badge and the Worshipful Master concludes his remarks with the words, '...whenever in correspondence with a Brother Mark Master Mason'.

Commentary: Continuing the remarks made at the outset of this commentary it is interesting that, as in the Craft, the Senior Warden, as the traditional ruler of a working Masonic lodge, still has the privilege of investing the new workman with his apron. In this case, as in the Royal Arch, the apron is referred to as a badge because in pre-Union days it was the practice to add another emblem, or badge, to one's Craft apron to indicate the different degrees to which one belonged. After the Union, each degree was required to have its own apron.

Similarly a jewel is presented with the apron and this, by reason of its shape and colour, certainly marks the further progress that this Mason has made in the science. It also ties in with the words of Scripture that preceded the Investiture for on the stone the distinctive mark of the new Mark Master Mason can be inscribed that, for this purpose, is 'a new name written which no man knoweth saving he that receiveth it'. That is not the original meaning of the verse but in the present case it fits very well. The jewel ever reminds us of the importance of the keystone whilst the other letters that it bears once more remind the recipient of the distinguished role of Hiram Abiff.

16th Pause: When the Worshipful Master has presented the working tools of the degree, the Charter and the Book of Constitutions and has said, '...whenever in correspondence with a Brother Mark Master Mason'.

Commentary: The working tools of this degree are those that appear early in our Masonic career but here they are referred to as operative items that enable a stone to be recognised as 'fitted for its place in the intended structure'.

That having been said the ritual then informs us that we are 'not meeting as operative masons but as Brethren engaged in speculative or symbolic Mark Masonry'. This is a very significant statement because it reminds us of the historical development of our organisation. It was originally a society of tradesmen formed to produce items for building use. Over the last 500 years it has been transformed into a society that uses operative items and terms but in a moral and allegorical sense. Thus, here, the maul and chisel repeat the lesson, first taught to Fellows but then transferred to a new Apprentice degree, of discipline and education. Such a lesson here leads to that approving mark of the Almighty as to fit us for our part in the creation of a house 'not made with hands, eternal in the heavens'.

It should occasion no surprise that we are now brought sharply down to earth as the lodge warrant, Book of Constitutions and the bye-laws of the lodge are presented. These, after all, are just as much the working tools of an Accepted Mark Master Mason. In some cases the bye-laws of the Province are also added.

17th Pause: At the end of the Advancement when the Worshipful Master has said, '...explaining the origin of the ceremony and signs'.

Commentary: In bringing the conferral of this degree, or two degrees in one, to its conclusion the Worshipful Master is expected to deliver an address of special quality. Here are voiced some of the finest words and most sublime precepts in the whole of today's Freemasonry. The danger is that, as usual, we hear and applaud the praises and sentiments but far too rarely do we reflect on what we repeatedly hear. Yet if anyone is to ask what the Mark degree has to offer it is to this final address that he needs to be directed.

Here we are called to act justly, to demonstrate mercy, to practice charity, to create and continue harmony, and live in unity with others as brethren. Here, too, we are assured that whatever troubles may assail us it is amongst Mark Master Masons that we can be sure to find friends who will assist us and bring us comfort. Not least we are to recall that central message of this degree that the stone which was rejected became the most important in the building. It is with that message echoing in our ears, if we will hear, that our ceremony closes and the new Mark Master Mason can take his place amongst us.

8

Commentary on the Holy Royal Arch Ceremony

This form of the Holy Royal Arch ceremony is intended for those times when there may be no candidate to be exalted, as an alternative to a plain rehearsal, or as further help in a Chapter of Instruction by providing new information about the various parts of the ceremony as they are presented.

As this is not a full rehearsal it is recommended that certain passages should be omitted. These are:
The preparation of the candidate by an Assistant Sojourner;
The obligation, save for the first line and last sentence;
The explanation of their ancestry given by the Principal Sojourner on the first entry to the Chapter, except for the first line and the last three lines;
Everything in the Principal Sojourner's account of discovery except the first and last sentences.

There are no lectures.

The explanations now follow and are prefaced by the phrases, '1st (2nd, etc) Pause' and the instruction indicating when an explanation is to be given. When that point occurs the Narrator will say 'pause' and read what follows under 'Commentary'. After each explanation, of course, work resumes.

During this presentation the only persons who take part are the officers previously appointed for the occasion. Everyone else remains seated throughout.

1st Pause: When the Scribe NEHEMIAH has repeated the qualifications of the candidate to MEZ and the candidate is admitted.

Commentary: The Passwords 'Ammi Ruamah', though they are now familiar to us, are, of course, substitutes for the original password that permitted access to this Order. That word was the one known only to Past Masters of the Craft. They were at one time the only persons usually qualified to enter the Royal Arch. When the Order was opened up to all Third Degree Masons after 1835 that word had to be dropped except for the entry to the third Principal's Chair. Needing a substitute password the Duke of Sussex is said to have consulted his friend the Chief Rabbi who suggested the present words as deriving from such daily Jewish readings as befitted the rest of the Royal Arch scripture passages.

2nd Pause: Following the prayer and affirmation of trust in T. T. A. L. G. M. H. after the MEZ says, 'Be seated, Companions'.

Commentary: Members of the Royal Arch are called Companions for three reasons:

a) As they were first called Brethren this term was eventually adopted to distinguish them from other Craft Freemasons.
b) The term means 'one who shares bread with another' and as the lodge custom up to the 19th Century was for ceremonies to be conducted around and beside a table, and interspersed with eating and drinking there, the term was a fitting one.
c) Initially the Royal Arch was a Christian ceremony linked with Church practice. The use of an Anglican Communion collect at the opening of the Chapter and the Gloria at the close preserves this link.

To call those who take part those who 'break bread together' was and still is strangely appropriate. It is also worth noting that the Royal Arch is the necessary step to the Knight Templar degree and the first requirement in that Order is to feed the new Knight Companion with bread and water.

3rd Pause: At the end of the perambulation and with the Candidate standing in front of the Sojourners.

Commentary: A perambulation is a regular feature of the Craft degrees. It is to enable the brethren in the North, East, South and West to check who is the candidate and that he is properly prepared. From an early period the route in the Chapter was by South, East, North and West, or a passage in a figure-of-eight. This emphasised to the candidate that he was in a new place and on a new journey. In the oldest Cambridge Chapter to this day the candidate is also made to step on the implements and feel the edge of the pedestal as he passes between the ensigns. The winding route, as in the old Mark ceremony that in some places preceded this, suggested a searching for something.

4th Pause: When the candidate stands before the arch or three stones after taking the required steps.

Commentary: Why do we take seven steps? The immediate answer is because these are the steps once taken in the Excellent/Super Excellent or Veils degree that often preceded the Exaltation, as it still does in Bristol. That ceremony has three steps to the Blue Veil, two steps to the Purple Veil, and two more to the Crimson Veil. These colours, of course, were those of the curtain covering the arched entrance to the Holy of Holies wherein the whole presence and nature of God was to be discovered. For candidates to take seven steps to the area of the pedestal is therefore very proper.

5th Pause: When the candidate has removed the arch stones.

Commentary: Some are puzzled as to why we wrench forth two arch stones when we are supposed to have arrived at the crown of a vaulted chamber. The answer is that we have here the joining of two different legends. One claimed that the ultimate secret was reached by the arches of Enoch, which is why some old Royal Arch tracing boards show a descent through nine arches to the crypt. Another legend claims that the object of our search was in a vaulted crypt where Hiram Abiff was buried, beneath the Holy of Holies. We thus retain mention of both arch and vault.

6th Pause: When the candidate has found the scroll.

Commentary: It is a 'scroll of vellum or parchment' and not a book that is found because we are trying to tell a tale from Old Testament times when documents were in such a form. You may know that to this day the Jewish scriptures are kept as parchment scrolls in a locked cabinet called a Tabernacle.

7th Pause: When the keystone has been removed.

Commentary: We now encounter the Keystone which has miraculously remained in place even though the two arch stones have been removed. This shows that what we are dealing with is allegory and not mere fact. The keystone is the chief stone of the Temple and is sometimes also called the cape-stone or cornerstone. It is not so much that the stone's removal allows access to the vault as that it lets the full light of God's word appear. We shall say more about that later.

8th Pause: When the candidate stands with the Volume of the Sacred Law on his upturned left hand and his right covering it.

Commentary: Before the days when there were ledges or desks to support the Volume of the Sacred Law (as there are still none in this ceremony) it was normal to hold the sacred writings in this fashion for an obligation. It is from this practice that the Scots to this day precede their salute in the Craft degrees with this sign. (Do it.)

9th Pause: After the Obligation and before sealing it.

Commentary: The title here used for the Deity is one that was introduced after 1835 to replace the Christian terms used in earlier practice. In using the words 'Most High' it clearly relates to the term used in the third degree and so underlines the Union agreement whereby the Holy Royal Arch was accepted as completing that step. It is at this point that we should also recall that when we are presented with our Royal Arch certificate the heading there shown is not the name that has just been used but the name of the Deity in Craft Masonry. The link between the two is again underlined.

10th Pause: When the Companions are holding the staves and the candidate has just had his hoodwink removed.

Commentary: The practice of tilting the staves with the ensigns inwards is because an attempt is being made to create the sense of a vaulted crypt. In some of the oldest Chapters in Yorkshire the members are each given white staves on their entry into the Chapter and these are used to form a symbolic roof instead of bending the ensign ones.

The sceptres forming a triangle were, of course, originally rods or staves and the Principals wore headgear that was related to what is now indicated on these items. The combining of the rods to form a right-angled triangle was actually the central secret of the medieval Master Mason/Architects – hence their problem when one of their number was absent.

11th Pause: When the MEZ has said, '...having exalted you into this Supreme Degree, so truly denominated the essence of Freemasonry'.

Commentary: The phrase 'Supreme Degree' used here might seem strange because we are firmly told elsewhere that the Royal Arch is not a degree but an Order. Moreover, when many are so aware of other so-called 'Higher Degrees' how can this step be called 'Supreme'? The answer is that when the Royal Arch was practised in the 18th Century it was considered to be a degree and as it purported to reveal a full knowledge of God and his true Name it came to be regarded as the 'Summum Bonum' or

Supreme Degree. It was just because most Christian elements of this Order were removed after 1835 that the other Christian Orders which had continued privately were now fully resumed and came to be regarded as 'higher'. For most Freemasons the Holy Royal Arch is and should be 'Supreme'.

12th Pause: When the passage from Genesis is read.

Commentary: This reading from the Book of Genesis is yet another indication of the de-Christianising of the Royal Arch. Originally the reading about Light was from the first verses of St. John's Gospel which was where the Volume of the Sacred Law was usually opened even in Craft lodges. Set in Old Testament times as the Royal Arch ceremony is, however, the present reading seems both fitting and natural. The Latin words 'FIAT LUX' that are seen on many Chapter arches refer to the words 'Let there be Light' that are recorded in Genesis chapter 1.

13th Pause: After the MEZ has enquired of the Sojourners, 'Strangers, whence come ye?' and the Principal Sojourner has replied.

Commentary: The form of address 'Most Excellent' not only honours the kingly figure typified by the first Principal but also reminds us that in order to reach that office one has first to be an Excellent Mason, which has hitherto meant passing through the Craft Chair. This distinction is emphasised by the words 'Excellent Companions' and 'Companions'. The term 'Most' points out that it is only when a Companion becomes a First Principal that the ultimate stage in the Royal Arch has been achieved.

14th Pause: When the Principal Sojourner has offered their 'assistance in that great and glorious undertaking'.

Commentary: The term 'Sojourner' is now used by us to refer solely to three of the Chapter officers but originally it described the three candidates who were required for a Royal Arch ceremony to take place, as is still the general requirement in North America. The term refers to someone who comes to stay for a time – the word deriving from the Latin 'diurnus' which then became French 'journée' meaning 'for a day'. This is related to the phrase 'journeyman mason' who was paid 'by the day'. The ritual phrase 'sojourn amongst you' meant that they offered casual labour and were not at first intending to stay.

15th Pause: After the explanation by the Principal Sojourner of their ancestry and ends with 'give peace to the whole earth.'

Commentary: The reason Cyrus seemed so ready to let the Jews and others return to their native land was because he thought that he would be better served by having his willing subjects working in their own countries rather than concentrated as prisoners in Babylon. To the Jews it seemed as if the prophecy of Isaiah was being fulfilled and they therefore interpreted it as their God influencing Cyrus's mind in their favour.

16th Pause: When the MEZ has said, 'You will communicate it to none but this august Sanhedrin'.

Commentary: The Sanhedrin was, as its Greek name suggests, a Council that 'sat together' to regulate the affairs of the Temple and the religious life of the Jews. It was composed of seventy elders together with a 'nasi' or president, and a scribe. If there was a vote which proved equally divided the High Priest was called in to give his casting vote, hence the notion of 72. The number 72 is now known to have had special architectural significance at the time our rituals were being formed. It is to this body that a new Royal Arch Companion is symbolically admitted at his investiture because a member of the Sanhedrin was called a 'Prince of the people' during his tenure.

17th Pause: As the Principal Sojourner reaches that part of their discovery where he says, '... the fragments which had fallen during the conflagration of the former Temple'.

Commentary: The passage or gallery here referred to is that which links up symbolically with those Arches of Enoch mentioned earlier. Yet whilst there were nine Arches of Enoch which fits with the nine persons needed to form a Chapter, only seven pairs of pillars are now mentioned which obviously connects with the seven steps in a Master's lodge.

18th Pause: When the Principal Sojourner has said, 'I was thus duly lowered into the vaulted chamber'.

Commentary: The procedure for visiting the underground vault was based on two accounts. One was the story of Philostorgius who told how workmen helping in the rebuilding of Jerusalem in the middle of the fourth century came across a cavity and were let down into it. The other account is the description in the Mishnah of how the High Priest was equipped with cords to allow him to move about in the darkness of the Sanctum Sanctorum and be drawn out by the priests outside the room if he was overcome by fainting or noxious vapours.

19th Pause: At the point in the Principal Sojourner's narrative where he says 'I was again lowered into the vault'.

Commentary: Mention of the keystone again raises the same issues that we faced earlier. A keystone only exists if there is an arch and here we are dealing with an underground vault. The Scots, of course, have their own solution and talk about a plug with many sides. The keystone was retained in England because originally the Royal Arch ceremony was preceded by a Mark ceremony in which the principal feature was a keystone that was first lost and then found and thus made possible the completion of the final arch of the Temple. Tradition dies hard so a keystone remains.

20th Pause: When the Principal Sojourner has described how 'a veil covered the face of the altar'.

Commentary: The white double-cube pedestal in front of us is symbolic of that found in the vault. In original Royal Arch working it was the central pedestal of the Lodge as it is now represented on the Royal Arch certificate, though then probably with a bowl of incense on the top. As it figuratively stands in the Holy Place, outside the Sanctum Sanctorum, it is said to be like the altar of incense described in the Volume of the Sacred Law as being in the Holy Place.

21st Pause: When the Principal Sojourner has asked to be excused from using the Sacred Name and has said, '...to make propitiation for the sins of the people'.

Commentary: The explanation of the original use of the cords used for descending into the vault is now more credible as we hear of the High Priest going once a year into the Holy of Holies to stand and pray before the Ark of the Covenant. Today only a very few Chapters still have an actual Ark of the Covenant standing before the pedestal but we should remember that the Ark is present on both our Craft and Royal Arch certificates. In the Veils ceremony it is the final item to be displayed there. It has also found a refuge in the Royal and Select Master degrees.

22nd Pause: When the MEZ has invested the candidate 'with the distinguishing badge of a Royal Arch Mason'.

Commentary: Notice that in the ritual here all the references are in the plural and so we say, 'The robes with which you are invested'. This is because, as was said earlier, there used to be three candidates. In older Yorkshire Chapters two of the Sojourners, once also the candidates, join the new Companion for the investiture. It certainly makes this part more intelligible.

Notice, too, that we speak not of an apron but of a badge. This is because originally a brother wore a Craft apron to which was now attached a badge showing that he was also an exalted Mason. After 1835 the new design of apron was approved and required but it was still called a badge.

23rd Pause: When the MEZ has said, 'the insignia of our Order'.

Commentary: Just to confuse us you should know that also in early times the Ribbon or Sash was described at the investiture as a 'Badge of honour'. You need not be surprised that it looks like a sword sash for in the 18th Century Freemasons often wore swords to use in the ceremonies, especially at the moment of obligation. It is worn on the left shoulder because the Volume of the Sacred Law informs us that at the erection of the second Temple the workers had the trowel in their right hand and the sword ready for their left hand in order to be able to defend themselves. Those who know the Royal Order of Scotland practice will confirm this as the ancient usage. The Royal Arch penalty, as if wielding the sword in the left hand, is thus also explained.

24th Pause: At the end of the investiture when the MEZ has said, '...you will by a regular gradation be admitted to an entire participation of our secrets'.

Commentary: We have already mentioned the use of staves in the Chapter but here we see the new Companion presented with his own staff as a member of the Sanhedrin. In medieval times all Princes were represented as holding rods and Moses, Prince of Egypt, did the same. The Master Mason on a building site also had a rod, along with his hat, robe and gloves. As Royal Arch Masons are now Architect Masons they have a staff as a sign of pre-eminence in the Craft. Later on the Principals in the Chapter would have a hat and robe though their hats have mostly been replaced by the emblem on the top of their sceptres. They are so distinguished because, despite what we may imagine, the Companions do not yet have all the Royal Arch secrets. They will only receive these as they occupy all the Principals' chairs.

25th Pause: When the Sacred Name has been shared with the new Companion.

Commentary: Only in the Royal Arch do we appreciate fully why the death of Hiram Abiff was so serious. It was not, as some may suppose, that the secret died with him but because what he knew was essential to complete the tripartite secret of the Grand Masters. That secret is now the Word of God (the Mason Word) that had to be shared to be correct. Once the secret also concerned three rods as was stated earlier.

26th Pause: When the MEZ has said, in his last address to the new Companion, 'the Providential means by which those ancient secrets were regained'.

Commentary: We take the present drama of the Chapter ceremony for granted. It was not always so. In the beginning what took place was that after an obligation and Charge the candidates were seated at the table and the three Principals required of the rest of the Companions in turn the answers to those questions of a catechism that told a similar story along with its meanings. Following that catechism the new Companions were invested and another Charge was delivered similar to that now often given at the close of the Chapter. The three Lectures that follow in our present ritual were only introduced after 1835.

9

Commentary on the Royal Arch Officers, Banners, Ensigns and Implements

This commentary on the officers, banners and implements that are connected with the Royal Arch ceremony is offered as a practical alternative to the rehearsal of an Exaltation. If the officers recite or read their own designated sections the other explanations can usually be undertaken by the rest of the Companions who are present. As an alternative procedure these explanations could be divided into three separate groups and given on three other occasions. When giving the explanations of a banner or ensign the speaker should hold, or point to, the item being described.

Zerubbabel

I am ZERUBBABEL. I am the first Principal of the Conclave, the name that we give to a meeting of a Royal Arch Chapter. The Chapter is the place where those who are fully qualified Master Masons meet to learn about and share the complete or supreme knowledge of 'The Mason's Craft'. Three Principals are needed to rule a Chapter because originally the revelation of the great Secret of construction was to know how to form a right-angled triangle as the basis of all design and erection. This needed three participants, each with a rod of different dimensions, which, when joined together created the required figure. That is why the absence or loss of one ruler meant that temporarily the 'secret was lost'. It is also why we three Principals each still have a rod or sceptre.

My name means 'God the Father in the East' and as the one I represent was a prince or leader of the Jewish people in exile in Babylon my rod bears a crown which reminds us of God's omnipotence. I was the one given authority by Cyrus, the Persian ruler, to lead the first group of Jewish people back to Canaan and Jerusalem where the city and temple were to be rebuilt. My task and responsibility, together with my co-Principals, is still to appoint suitable people to the work and to reveal to them the full knowledge that we share in a Chapter.

Haggai

I am HAGGAI. I am the second Principal appointed to rule in the Chapter. As the first Principal has told you I possess a part of the ancient knowledge that is peculiar to a Conclave. It may interest you to know that in some old Chapters it is still customary for all present to form threes when opening and closing a Chapter, just as we Principals do. That was to prove that all those present were fully qualified members. It was also to remind the Companions of the princely, prophetic and priestly aspects of our Order by so taking part.

My name, meaning 'festive', refers to one of the books of the Bible and one of my roles is that of a prophet. That is why the rod that I bear carries an 'All Seeing Eye' that symbolically represents the omnipresence of the Almighty. My role after the return of the Jews from exile in Babylon was that of scribe and I acted in that capacity in the first Sanhedrin that was set up after we had settled again in Jerusalem.

The Sanhedrin was the council set up to govern the people of Israel and was composed of six persons from each of the twelve tribes. One of those representatives was the prince that presided over the Sanhedrin and another was the Scribe who recorded their decisions. If a deciding vote had to be given the High Priest was brought in to do so. Thus all those present as our Principals were needed to conclude essential business.

Joshua

I am JOSHUA. I am the third Principal who assists in ruling the Chapter.

My name means 'the God who saves' and my role is not only that of a priest but of a High Priest. It is I, and not my father Josedech, who has that honour. That is why the rod that I bear has a 'mitre' at its head. In earlier days, and still in a few English Chapters, the person in my chair wore a breastplate that had twelve jewels representing the twelve tribes of Israel, like the ensigns. Incidentally the three Principals used to wear as headgear the items now represented on their rods.

The mitre and breastplate of the third Principal represent the omniscience of the Almighty who has entrusted to his people, and us the priests in particular, the sacred knowledge of the Scriptures, prayers and ceremonies that God revealed to Israel. That is why it is usually my responsibility to pray and read passages from the Volume of the Sacred Law at our meetings.

It is no coincidence that the name that this Principal bears is the same in Hebrew as that which we know as Jesus. For in the earlier days of this Order its Christian significance was paramount and there was much in the ritual about Jesus as the High Priest entering the Holy of Holies to make atonement for the sins of the people. That is why the use of the cords for being lowered into the sacred vault referred to that priestly practice.

Ezra

I am SCRIBE EZRA. In the Scriptural account I was the leader of the second group of Israelites who returned to Jerusalem. Much of the building of the next Temple had been completed by the time I arrived so that my task was to ensure the restoration of the Law of Moses as that which was taught and followed by those attached to the Temple, whether as its servants or its attendants. That is why in our Conclave lectures I am described as an 'expounder of the Sacred Law'. My name means 'help'.

The work was especially necessary because the returned exiles had become used to speaking and writing in the Chaldee tongue and they now had to become familiar once more with the original Hebrew text of the Scriptures. It is interesting to learn that though Ezra taught the people Hebrew he wrote what was to be taught in the Chaldean alphabet.

Because Ezra was a learned person who sought to instruct the people in the holy scriptures it is not surprising that in English Chapters he still wears a surplice, the dress of a speaker or teacher in the Established Church of this land. The white of his clothing also relates to what was once the white veil that was reached when the three other veils ceremony ended and that divided the candidate from the Holy of Holies where the three Principals were meant to be seated. To further represent this veil many Chapters require the Scribes to stand by the easternmost staves when the candidate is being obligated.

Nehemiah

I am SCRIBE NEHEMIAH. I was the leader of the third group of Jews returning to Jerusalem. In exile I had been the king's cup-bearer, or the one who tested what he might drink before he did so. On my return I was also, like Scribe Ezra, appointed an officer of the Sanhedrin and given the role of a Scribe.

My name means 'God's consolation' and my task was to superintend the rebuilding of the walls of Jerusalem so that the Temple and people might be safe from the attacks of those who resented the return of the exiles' descendants. Some of these opponents were the Samaritans and that is why there was conflict between them and the Jews for centuries afterwards.

The distinction of my office is marked, as explained for Ezra, by the wearing of a surplice and this garb of a teacher should remove any notion of my office being the Chapter equivalent of an Inner Guard, wherever I may be placed. My duty is to assist the Scribe Ezra and in some Chapters it is further marked by our doing the veiling and unveiling of the pedestal rather than by the Principals. In any case it is our privilege to equip the men who are engaged for the work of clearing the new Temple's ground and then further preparing them for their investiture. It is not a menial but a respected office and Scribe Nehemiah is the first officer of the Conclave seen by any candidate as he is admitted.

Principal Sojourner

I am the PRINCIPAL SOJOURNER. I am nowadays an officer of the Chapter but as my name suggests I originally represented someone who came from outside and requested the opportunity to 'sojourn', or spend days, in the company of the Companions and assist them in their labours. At one stage in the 18th Century the candidates were called 'the sojourners' and as three candidates were required for the ceremony, as is still the case in some parts of the United States of America, the idea of three sojourners began.

At this point the obligated candidates once simply listened to a lecture but as the ceremony developed the need for three more officers became evident. In the Chapters held in the Antients' lodges there was the Excellent (or Super Excellent) Master degree that is more popularly known as the 'Ceremony of the Veils'. In that ceremony I was known as the Captain of the Third Veil. It was as one passed through that veil that the first mention of God's true names was given. After 1834 this ceremony was discontinued in England and the form that is presently practised was established. As you will know my role is that of the discoverer of the secrets in the vault but it has always to be remembered that I do this on behalf of the candidate so my old role in that position is in part restored. What might seem strange is that, as in the West of a lodge, it is my privilege to close the Chapter. An ancient link with Craft working is thus retained.

First Assistant Sojourner

I am the FIRST ASSISTANT SOJOURNER. My traditional task, as hinted by the Principal Sojourner, was to offer my services as one of the Israelites returning from Babylon, to help reconstruct the Temple in Jerusalem that was destroyed by the Assyrians. As you have also been told there was a time before 1834 when another degree was practised before the actual Exaltation. The degree was conducted in three parts, each of which were separated by one of three curtains coloured blue, purple and crimson. These colours are still recalled by the colours of the robes of the three Principals. I was appointed to be in charge of the second or purple curtain and was known as the Captain of the Second Veil. Within the area behind that veil candidates were reminded of the encounter between Moses and the Pharaoh who ruled Egypt, prior to the release of the Hebrews from that land. It may be noted that this Veils ceremony emphasises the idea of release from exile that is still a theme retained in our current practice. It may also be of interest to learn that in Scotland it is the custom for the officer in my position to be the one who is lowered into the vault rather than the principal Sojourner. Whether that means that I am more easily dispensed with or that the Principal Sojourner must remain in charge of the operation is not disclosed.

Second Assistant Sojourner

I am the SECOND ASSISTANT SOJOURNER, though in some places I am called the Junior Assistant Sojourner. Mention has already been made of why there are three of us and of other duties which we had to perform in the late eighteenth and early nineteenth centuries Those tasks are still performed in Bristol where a Ceremony of the Veils was allowed to be reintroduced almost a century ago. It may be of interest to learn that in West Yorkshire today there is a Chapter that uses the older and much longer opening ritual that involves the questioning by the MEZ of each of the officers as to what are their several duties. In my case the answer that is there to be given is 'The Captain of the First Veil' and the duty of that office is 'To guard that veil and allow none to pass without giving the word and grip of that veil and to report the same to the Captain of the Third Veil'. Thus is retained the memory of the older form of part of Royal Arch Masonry even though there is not the least semblance of a veil in that Chapter today. Such practice reminds us of the antiquity of our ceremonies and the fact that my office, like others, is not here by chance. Even our name of Sojourner helps us to realise that whilst Sojourners may first have been temporary visitors they are now necessary parts of the whole Exaltation process.

Judah

I am holding the ensign of JUDAH. In Hebrew the meaning of the name Judah is 'Praise', and this agrees with the words of Genesis chapter 9 where Jacob called his sons together so that he could tell each of them what was to happen. Jacob says: 'Judah, your brothers shall praise you; your hand shall be upon the neck of your enemies; your father's sons shall bow down before you'. As Judah was to be the principal tribe of the Jewish people it is hardly surprising that, when next referred to, it is as a noble lion. 'Judah, you are a lion's cub; from the prey, my son, you return, and like a lion you crouch and lie down, like a lioness whom one fears to rouse'. And Jacob continues: 'The sceptre shall not depart from Judah, nor the ruler's staff from between his feet until he comes to whom it belongs'.

That is why we always see on this ensign a lion with a sceptre beneath its feet and sometimes a crown above it. The royal house of David descended from Judah. Some Latin words beneath the shield (Vivat Leo De Tribu Juda) mean 'Long live the Lion of the tribe of Judah' though there is another phrase (Accubuit ut leo) meaning 'He lay down like a lion'. The Talmud says that as Jacob's body was carried to burial it had a sceptre and a crown of gold laid upon it.

Issachar

I am holding the ensign of ISSACHAR. In Hebrew the name Issachar means 'A man who is a reward' or 'A man who is rewarded'. How can this fit with what Jacob says in Genesis 49, 'Issachar is a strong ass lying down between two burdens', which is at least the picture before us and fits one of the usual Latin inscriptions (Intra Onera Accumbens)? An answer begins to be clear as we learn that the tribe of Issachar was originally meant to possess a rich area of land as reward but the tribe was indolent and eventually agreed to sit down and suffer the indignity of paying tribute to others rather than fight their enemies. Though the ass is usually a sign of physical strength it here appears to give way, bends its back under the loads that would be put on it and is then forced to work as a slave who is then but meagrely rewarded. In Genesis chapter 30, Leah, Jacob's wife, says, 'God has given me my reward because I gave my slave to my husband'. So she named the son so raised Issachar, the man who was, at least in that situation, a reward. The Latin phrase that sometimes appear beneath this ensign is 'Giving way (or is it, Giving up) between limits' (Accubans inter terminos). Is it surprising that this is one of the Hebrew tribes least heard of? In the High Priest's breastplate the jewel representing this tribe was the amethyst.

Zebulon

I am holding the ensign of ZEBULON. The Hebrew name means 'a place where one dwells'. This fits very well the words that are spoken by Jacob to his son in Genesis chapter 49. What he says there is: 'Zebulon shall dwell by the shore of the sea and he shall be a haven for ships; and his border shall extend as far as Sidon'. This explains very satisfactorily why there are pictures of ships on the shield that is displayed. Moreover, whichever of the alternative Latin phrases is used its meaning adds naturally to the messages that we have already had. One of these readings (In litore maris habitabit) is 'He shall dwell on the shore of the sea' whilst the other runs: 'As a safe haven for ships he is himself such a harbour'. The words in each case refer to the favourable geographical position of the territory that was allotted to be this tribe's place of habitation. It was one that permitted sailing vessels to find a safe berth and yet also sail away without difficulty. Moses later said of this tribe of Zebulon, 'They will feast on the abundance of the sea and the treasures hidden in the sand'.

It has also to be noticed that an alternative name for this tribe was ZABULON, which term was once early associated with our Holy Royal Arch as it signified the place where the Almighty came to dwell on the Ark of the Covenant in the Holy of Holies of the Tabernacle and Temple. The term not being thus properly understood as the 'safe haven' of God's people was later changed to Jabulon. In that form it is now never used in our Chapter ceremonies.

Reuben

I am holding the ensign of REUBEN. In Hebrew the name means 'Behold, a son'. This is fully supported by the words used by Jacob in Genesis 49: 'Reuben, thou art my first-born, my might and the beginning of my strength, excelling in honour and excelling in power'. This may seem to have nothing to do with the waves of the sea and the Latin (Aquarum instar ruens) on the ensigns that represent this tribe but further on in the Bible this is what we discover: 'Turbulent as the waters, you will not excel; because you went up onto your father's bed, on to my couch and defiled it'.

Like the waves Reuben's conduct is stormy and unpredictable. His instability is like the overflowing waters that can break all restraints and this is said to reflect this son's haughty and arrogant attitude as the eldest child, or even some lack of self-control and firmness of purpose on his part. The reference to usurping his father's bed was also based on the Bible passage in Genesis 35, verse 22, where he is supposed to have slept with Bilhah, his father's mistress. The Latin words given above mean also 'Rushing like waters' but there is another (Primogenitus meus) 'My firstborn'.

Simeon

I am holding the ensign of SIMEON. This name in Hebrew means 'Hearing'. Simeon is usually linked with Levi as the words of Jacob when he called the sons together makes clear: 'Simeon and Levi are brothers – their swords are weapons of violence. Let me not enter their council nor join their assembly, for they killed men in their anger and at their pleasure they have hamstrung oxen.' This all refers to the murderous attack that the Simeonites and Levites made on the people of Shechem and the weapons that they employed because of what Jacob calls 'their anger for it was fierce and their wrath which was so cruel'. It is not surprising, therefore, that on this ensign there is a sword or scimitar crossed with a dagger or a sharp knife. The Jewish writings or Midrash say that Simeon's device was really a city, meaning Shechem, and some old Chapters still have this displayed on their standard. The usual Latin phrase (Vasa iniquitatis bellantia) means 'Implements for fighting injustice' though some ensigns have the alternative (Dividam et dispergam) 'I will divide and scatter' because these words appear in Genesis chapter 49. The tribe's jewel was a topaz.

Gad

I am holding the ensign of GAD. This name in Hebrew means 'a troop or a marauding band' and that fits perfectly with the words of Jacob: 'A gang of raiders shall attack him, but he will pursue them at their heels'. This accords with the historic record for the tribe of Gad succeeded in expelling the Ammonites, the Moabites and the Ephraimites who constantly raided their borders.

You will not be surprised to learn that the Jephthah mentioned in our second degree belonged to this tribe of Gad for Gad was famed for courage and success in war.

It is perfectly fitting, therefore, that the emblem representing this tribe is a troop of horses with riders and sometimes their pennants display a lion, for Moses said of Gad 'He lives like a lion, tearing at arm and leg'. The Midrash described Gad's device as a camp or tent and so that picture sometimes appears. The Latin words (Ipse tandem devincit) of this ensign mean 'He at last will subdue' though occasionally you read 'The Troop will be destroyed but not him'. The jewel of this tribe is a jacinth.

Ephraim

I am holding the ensign of EPHRAIM. The name in Hebrew means 'Doubly fruitful' and this is especially appropriate because it fits the division of the tribe of Joseph into those of his children, Ephraim and Manasseh, the latter is next in this presentation. This is what was referred to by Jacob in Genesis chapter 49. Since Reuben had been so unruly his double portion was granted to Joseph.

The beast on this ensign refers to the words of Moses in Deuteronomy 33: 'In majesty he is like a firstborn bull; his horns are the horns of a wild ox, and with them he will gore the nations even unto the ends of the earth'. Another translation reads: 'His horns are like the horns of unicorns' and that is why some ensigns display that creature on them. The Latin inscription (Amans triturare) means 'Fond of threshing' that probably refers to the idea of this tribe trampling like a bullock upon the corn and lands of others.

Manasseh

I am holding the ensign of MANASSEH. This name means 'to cause forgetfulness'. This was a fitting reference either to Jacob's seemingly forgetting that Manasseh is the elder son of Joseph or to the need of Manasseh to forget that his younger brother had been the first to receive Jacob's blessing. This mix up is confirmed by the Midrash that states that the device of Manasseh should be a wild ox or an unicorn, though this last symbol has, as we have seen, been taken by Ephraim. The device now used follows the other words of Jacob when addressing all his sons: 'He (Manasseh) is a fruitful vine, near a spring, whose branches climb over a wall'. What we sometimes see shown is a palm tree because that accords with the words of Moses: 'May their land (that of Manasseh) be blessed with unripened fruit, rich with the best fruits of each season'. The Latin (Ramus fecundus juxta fontem) on this ensign conveys this message: 'A fruitful bough close to a well or spring'. Manasseh's jewel was an onyx.

Benjamin

I am holding the ensign of BENJAMIN. The name translated from Hebrew means 'Son at the right hand' and following the disappearance of Joseph which Jacob for so long thought to mean his death, Benjamin became the child most loved. This is also reflected in the words of Moses found in Deuteronomy chapter 33, 'Let the beloved of the Lord always rest secure in Him, for He shields him all the day long and the one whom the Lord loves rests upon his breast. '

Yet Jacob's words in Genesis 49 are also clear: 'He is as a ravenous wolf that in the morning devours its prey, and in the evening divides the plunder'. This referred to the warlike nature of this tribe and that is why a wolf is usually seen on this ensign. There is a different ensign in Sunderland on which there is no wolf but there are horsemen who brandish weapons, thus confirming the warlike characteristics that are mentioned by Jacob. The Latin words associated with this ensign (Manus comedit praedam et vesperi dividet spolia), mean 'In the morning he eats the prey and at evening divides the spoil'. The jewel of this tribe was a jasper.

Dan

I am holding the ensign of DAN. His name when translated from the Hebrew means 'a judge' and this fits perfectly what Jacob says in Genesis 49: 'Dan will provide justice for his people as one of the tribes of Israel'. Yet other words of scripture also fit the emblem on this ensign for we read: 'Dan will be a serpent by the roadside and a viper along the path that bites the horse's heels so that its rider tumbles backwards'. Sometimes the ensigns representing Dan showed just a horned viper that hid itself in the sand and bit whatever disturbed it, but the Midrash speaks of the sign of Dan as it is described in Moses's words: 'Dan is a lion's cub springing out of Bashan'. Yet again there are other ensigns that show an eagle with a serpent in its claws but this reference is to the alternative connections of the twelve tribes with the signs of the Zodiac. In that connection the tribe of Dan was associated with the sign of Capricorn that could be represented by a flying eagle with a serpent in its talons. The Latin words used here (Coluber in via) mean 'A snake on the road' but some have an alternative that reads: 'Rising up close to the road is that which feeds upon a horseman'.

Asher

I am holding the ensign of ASHER. The Hebrew name here means 'Happy' and this fits Moses's words in Deuteronomy 33: 'Most blessed of sons is Asher who is favoured by his brothers and is able to bathe his feet in soothing oil'. There is, however, another sense in which happiness could be attributed to this tribe because its territory was a very abundant one producing the choicest fruits as well as the necessities of life. Thus it is that Jacob says in Genesis 49: 'Asher's food will be rich: he will provide delicacies fit for a king'. The emblem on this ensign is thus either a flourishing tree or a golden goblet or urn. The tree is probably meant to be an olive that gives the oil mentioned earlier, whilst the vessels are those used for storing the same substance which has always been a symbol of fruitfulness and plenty. The Latin words (Prebebit delicias regibus) mean 'He will provide delicacies for kings'. The tribal jewel here is an agate.

Naphthali

I am holding the ensign of NAPHTHALI. The meaning of the Hebrew name here is 'to wrestle' or 'to struggle' and one aspect of this tribe is suggested by Jacob's words to his sons: 'Naphthali is a doe that after struggle is set free and that bears beautiful fauns'. The tribe would struggle to gain freedom and be able to produce attractive offspring. Moreover, Jacob's words explain why the emblem on this standard is a lively doe or hind.

The richness and fertility of the land that was occupied by this tribe is again emphasised by Moses's words: 'Naphthali is abounding with the favour of the Lord, is full of blessing and will inherit the territory south to the lake'. The Latin words used with this ensign (Cerva emissa) mean 'A hind let loose' or 'Behold, a deer that gives birth'. The jewel in the High Priest's breastplate for this tribe was an emerald.

The Lion Banner

This, the first of the principal banners, that displays a LION, is so placed in the Book of Numbers chapter 2 verse 2. As we have already discovered in this presentation the lion was the emblem of Judah, the tribe which was to produce the royal line of David and Solomon. In the Book of Numbers we also read that Judah's companies were to be placed in the East, towards the point of the sunrise, when the Israelites made camp in the wilderness of Sinai. That, in current Masonic terms, certainly indicates a position of rule and majesty. The colour portrayed on this first banner is crimson or blood red and this agrees with more of the words used by Jacob in Genesis chapter 49: 'Judah will tether his donkey to a vine, washing his garments in wine and his robes in the blood of grapes'. This also fits in with the colour of the carbuncle jewel which represented Judah in the High Priest's breast-plate. The later connection of the lion with St. Mark was because the gospel bearing his name begins with the words, 'The voice of one roaring in the wilderness'.

The Man Banner

This, the second principal banner, bears another representative emblem of the tribe of Reuben. In this case the symbol used is totally different to that of the 'waves' that we saw earlier. This, however, is just as appropriate because it was then noted that the name Reuben meant 'Behold a son' and Jacob's words in Genesis chapter 49 are similar: 'This is my first born, my might, the first sign of my strength'. It is therefore hardly surprising that such words might suggest the figure of a MAN.

What can be a matter of great interest when visiting another Chapter is discovering the type of man that is shown in each case. Since the words of

Jacob include the following: 'You shall not excel because you went up to my couch and defiled it' the man on this banner is sometimes shown partially naked with but a scanty cloak, and hence sometimes it looks like John the Baptist. Other figures look like a king or prophet and this is also appropriate because, as this symbol was later used to represent St. Matthew, who told the story of God becoming man amongst the Jews, it is right to see this figure as a teacher or leader.

The colour connected with this banner was flesh-coloured or pink-red and this linked up with the cornelian stone in the High Priest's breastplate.

The Ox Banner

The third principal banner relates to the tribe of Ephraim, that camped in the West, and therefore, like the ensign of this same tribe that we encountered previously it bears the figure of an OX. The words of Moses in Deuteronomy chapter 33 point out that the creature that was their symbol was sometimes a bull, a bullock or even a calf. These animals, just because they represented creatures of great strength, were those that were frequently chosen for sacrifice on the great altar of the Temple at Jerusalem. It was this fact that linked the ox with the Gospel writer, St. Luke, since he was the one who specially told the story of the sacrifice of Christ.

The colour associated with Ephraim was dark or bluey green and this linked up, as we learnt earlier, with a jasper. The green colour also relates to the further blessing that was associated with the sons of Joseph: 'the choicest fruits of the sun and the finest produce of the ancient mountains'.

The Eagle Banner

The fourth and last of the principal banners is one which displays an EAGLE. Since this banner is representative of the tribe of Dan it may at first seem strange that this symbol is so different from that which we saw earlier, a horseman whose steed is attacked by a serpent. Yet it may also be remembered that there was mention of the connection with the Zodiac sign of Capricorn, an eagle with a serpent in its grasp.

There is another passage in Genesis chapter 48 verse 18 where we read: 'I look for your deliverance, O Lord', and this comes at the end of the section relating to Dan. This has been linked in the past with Moses's words in Deuteronomy where he says: 'The Most High shielded him and cared for him, like an eagle that alerts its nest and hovers over its young, spreading its wings to catch them and carry them on its pinions'. The link of the eagle with St. John the Evangelist may relate to several themes: the good news brought to God's brood as if by a flying angel, or to the heavenward ascension of Christ; or even, as has been said, when the eagle holds a serpent in its claws, thus signifying the conquest of good over evil. The colour of this banner is light green, for the tribal stone as worn by the High Priest was a sapphire.

The Triple Tau

Here we have the TRIPLE TAU which may be described as the true distinguishing mark of the Holy Royal Arch. The requirement of a 'mark' is not here accidental because all those who were true Master Masons in earlier days had already passed through what we now call the Mark degrees and had been provided with their special and personal Mark. The Tau is certainly a mark of 'perfect life', as we are taught in this Order from the Book of Ezekiel. Bearing in mind, however, the original association of this Order with Moses, a possible Egyptian reference is not out of place. The 'T' form of this Mark was exactly the same as that of the instrument known as a Nilometer, which was placed beside that great river at the time of its annual flooding. If the water reached the crossbar then irrigation was assured and the crops providing food for the whole population was again assured. The Tau has also a reference to the Cross. The Romans made a convicted criminal carry the cross beam to the place of execution and then that beam was laid on top of the upright stake that was already fixed in the ground. The notice of the prisoner's crime was then sometimes nailed to the back of the cross beam, thus giving the outline with which most of us are familiar. The Tau has the true shape of the cross itself. The union of the three taus corresponds at least to the idea of the three Principals uniting for their proper communication of the Royal Arch secrets.

The Trowel

This is the TROWEL. Since the trowel was eventually a sign of a Passed Master, who was thus recognised as fit to assist in completing the building of the Second Temple, and only such Masons were originally admitted as Companions, it is not surprising that the Trowel figures prominently amongst the implements on the floor of the Chapter room.

During the reconstruction of the sacred edifice and the walls of Jerusalem there was always a danger of interruption or attack by those who wanted to prevent this work being carried out. Accordingly we are informed that those engaged on the building work were to have their trowel in one hand and their sword or weapon of defence ready to use with the other. The trowel being the implement that applied the mortar that binds the building units together was recognised as a symbol of brotherly or companionable unity. It was also a sign of confidentiality in so far as the secrets of a brother would be equally well preserved and cemented in his breast. It is not surprising that the tool of the Worshipful Masters, as also of the early initiates, was a trowel.

The Sword

This is the SWORD. We have already heard that this implement was necessary at the rebuilding of the Temple and walls of Jerusalem and its introduction into our Order was part of enacting that scriptural situation. The fact that one is made a Prince and ruler when invested in the Royal Arch meant that in the 18th Century such an implement would also fit the rank of such a person. The sword even began to replace the trowel in the Craft. The fact that the sword was presumed to be held in the left hand, as the trowel was in the right, helps to explain why the sash that may once have held a sword is on the right; why the penalty in this Order is given with the left hand, as if holding a sword; and why the toast to our Grand Originals is given with the left hand.

The presence of a sword, as that wielded by a worthy defender of the holy places, also explains how easy it was to link the Royal Arch with what was once its immediate partner, the Knight Templar degree. Since all Knights Templar had, in the medieval Order, to be of noble blood the idea of

Princes and Rulers in this Order made their holders very natural candidates.

The Janitor

I am (or represent) the JANITOR. The principle of having someone to keep the meeting places of Freemasons private and safe meant that every part of the Society had its own officers to discharge this task. In the 18th Century, whether the Royal Arch was conducted as part of the Craft practice, as with the Antients, or as a separate but attached practice of some lodge members, the person who kept the outer door was the same Tyler for both. When the Royal Arch was organised separately from the Craft, and especially after 1834, a new title was given to the keeper of the outer door. He was now called the Janitor. The term was an appropriate one in Freemasonry for it derives from the same Roman God, Janus, with two faces, who gave his name to January, the month that looks back on the past year and looks forward to the new. The Janitor is the one who, while keeping a wary eye out for strangers and intruders is also expected to care for the new candidate as he prepares for his fresh experiences in the Chapter. Having their old Craft lodge connection firmly in mind some old Chapters today still have an Outer Janitor and an Inner one. This is not a tradition that ought to be maintained for it is hoped that the status of the Scribe Nehemiah, already described, needs to be recognised as being of more significance than a mere doorkeeper.

A Glossary of Royal Arch Terms and their Pronunciation

Ammonites .... Amm'-on-ites
Asher .... Ash'-er
Bashan .... Bay'-shan
Bilhah .... Bill'-hah
Canaan .... Kay'-nan
Chaldean .... Kal'-de-an
Cyrus .... Cy'-russ
Deuteronomy .... Dew'-ter-on'-om-y
Ephraim .... Ee'frame
Ephraimites .... Ee'frame-ites'
Ezekiel .... E-zeek'-iyel
Ezra .... Ez'-ra
Genesis .... Jen'-es-is
Haggai .... Hag'-eye
Israel .... Iz'-ray-el
Israelites .... Iz'-ray-el-ites
Issachar .... Iss'-a-car
Jephthah .... Jeff'-thah
Josedech .... Joe'-ze-deck
Joshua .... Josh'-oo-ar
Judah .... Jew'-dah
Leah .... Lee'-ah
Levi .... Lee'-vie
Levites .... Lee'-vites
Manasseh .... Man-ass'-eh
Midrash .... Mid'-rash
Moabites .... Mow'-ab-ites

Naphtli ....Naff'-ta-lee
Nehemiah ....Nay'-he-my'-yah
Reuben ....Rue'-ben
Sanhedrin ....San-head'-rin
Shechem ....Sheck'-em
Sidon ....Sigh'-don
Simeon ....Sim'-e-on
Simeonites ....Sim'-e-on-ites'
Talmud ....Tal'-mood [*to rhyme with* good]
Zebulon ....Zeb'-oo-lon
Zerubbabel ....Zer-rub'-bab-el

SD - #0026 - 070726 - C0 - 210/148/5 - PB - 9780853182719 - Gloss Lamination